FREE HELP

from Uncle Sam to Start
Your Own Business

FREE HELP

from Uncle Sam
to Start Your
Own Business
(Or Expand the One You Have)

Fifth Edition
Completely Revised

William Alarid

Puma Publishing Company
Santa Maria, California

FREE HELP from Uncle Sam

First Printing, May 1988
Second Printing, August 1988
Third Printing, November 1988
Fourth Printing, July 1989 (completely revised)
Fifth Printing, October 1989
Sixth Printing, June 1990
Seventh Printing, August 1991
Eighth Printing, February 1992 (completely revised)
Ninth Printing, January 1994
Tenth Printing, August 1995
Eleventh Printing, May 1997 (completely revised)
Twelfth Printing, October 2000 (completely revised)

Library of Congress Cataloging-in-Publication Data

Alarid, William M., 1936–
    Free help from Uncle San to start your own business
    (or expand the one you have)/
William Alarid.—5th ed., completely rev.
        p. cm.
Includes index.
    1. Small business—Government policy—United States—Handbook,
manuals, etc. 2. New business enterprises—United States—Handbooks,
manuals, etc. I. Title

HD2346.U5 A63 2000
338.6420973—dc21   00-044564

ISBN 0-940673-75-4

Acknowledgments

Sidney Lawrence, in Washington, DC, researched much of the new material in this edition.

Gail Kearns did her usual superb job of editing, Christine Nolt the typesetting, and Robert Howard designed the cover.

CONTENTS

Contents

Contents

Contents

Contents

Contents

Contents

Introduction

In down times or up times, entrepreneurship goes on and on and on like The Energizer. There always are and always will be those who say "to hell with prognosticators." These men and women see an opportunity, an opening in the economic fabric of our nation, and they jump into it with both feet, or head first. Never mind that only 80 percent of them will survive the first five years.

The true entrepreneur is a bit of a gambler, but a concerned and calculating gambler. The more knowledgeable he or she is, the greater his or her chances of survival. Knowledge, then, is the ace in the hole. Money? Sure, that's important too. Money is vital as a lubricant, but it's not the driver that steers the vehicle. The entrepreneur is the driver, and it is knowledge and all the human characteristics that make up the complex and somewhat mysterious entrepreneur, that first of all motivates him or her.

Money comes next. And that's the topic we take on in this book. Much money flows from one of the thousand agencies and offices of the federal government and that of the 50 states. Not that Uncle Sam's money is a leaky faucet—quite the contrary. Money from Uncle Sam is getting more difficult to tap—but not impossibly so. It just takes know-how and know-who.

Throughout the 5th edition of *Free Help from Uncle Sam*, we've trod on the side of fiscal conservatism. The sources you find listed and the suggestions we've made are realistic and pragmatic ones. We've tried to avoid the blue sky and rose-colored glasses that some books focus on.

Uncle Sam's money, don't forget, is our money. The only source of income for the treasury of the United States is your and my taxes.

As the custodian of our money, our government is charged with dispensing --investing, if you will—some of that money in viable private businesses. In order to get that money, you in private enterprise must regard the source as realistically and honestly as you do the neighborhood bank.

The government, on the other hand, has become more banker-like, since those lush days of free and easy money during past years. Now commercial bank refusals, financial statements, valid collateral, pragmatic cash flow schedules, and a credible payback plan must accompany every application for Uncle Sam's money (that is, our money!). There are few exceptions. Normally, you wouldn't want those "exceptions"—disabilities, disasters, and dramatic social disadvantages—that could result in direct government loans at lower interest rates. However, in these exigencies, such loans do exist and it's only right that you should know about them.

In this 5th edition we have also emphasized more and new case histories and success stories. Few portions of a written record are as inspirational and stimulating as actual life happenings from which you can draw experience and incentives. Also, included for you are new contacts, updated addresses, and phone numbers, which are accurate up to publication time.

More emphasis has also been placed on entrepreneurial areas that are growing—such as international trade (primarily export) and minority enterprises.

You should also be advised of some new trends. More and more men and women in their middle years are getting their "parachutes" and are floating to earth without a preconceived place to land. These folks are squeezed out by increasing corporate mergers. Many of them are mid- to upper-level executives who, instead of the proverbial gold watch, are sent into temporary "retirement" with a sizable pension fund poke or financial settlement. Members of the Armed Forces and even longtime employees of Civil Service are taking early retirement. In most cases these men and women take with them profound skills and accumulated fiscal security. Many of them will apply these twin assets to new businesses, or to the acquisition of existing businesses. Sometimes these skills and contacts can even be converted into doing business with their former employers.

Approximately 750,000 entrepreneurs will start a business this year. Most of them follow their dreams regardless of the risks inherent in entrepreneurship. However, you should be mindful of the reality that the businessperson who minimizes the risk is the one who is going to survive—and prosper—the longest and best. Usually, inspiration, enthusiasm, motivation, hard work and persistence are great propellants. Knowledge, nonetheless, is the glue that holds them all together. Money is the great lubricant that keeps them all flowing. Much of that funding comes from and flows through U.S. agencies and state governments.

How to get some of that help, where to get, and from whom to get, is the job of *Free Help from Uncle Sam...*

It's up to you now to find the right reference and to follow the rules. Be complete, be realistic, and be professional about your contact and follow-up. Be patient, too. The U.S. Government is a vast bureaucracy, sometimes staffed by brilliant fellow-citizens, sometimes by petty bureaucrats and time wasters who are just waiting for pension-time. Often it seems like all that red tape is not worth the effort, but remember that it's your money you are applying for—and the purpose of your request must be to generate profits and benefits for you and yours and for your fellow citizens.

William Alarid

About the Author

William Alarid is an entrepreneur who has used government aid to start several small businesses. He's the author of two business books. Alarid is an engineer, a member of *Mensa*, and is listed in *Who's Who in California*. He resides in Santa Maria, California, with his wife, Casey, his daughter, Christine, and his son, David.

CHAPTER 1

Success Stories About Some of Uncle Sam's Citizens

With 1,000 different loan programs, two dozen agencies, and congressionally mandated "ombudsman" departments in every federal agency (most of them designed to help under-privileged and minorities to get a fair shake), success stories reported by the SBA and its supported agencies (SCORE, SBDC, SBIR, et al.) dominate the news. Often overlooked, however, are success stories from other agencies such as the Department of Commerce, Department of Agriculture, and Department of Energy. Here are a few from which you might draw helpful inspirations. Taking advantage of them can save you many $$$.

An Entrepreneur with a Nose for Opportunity

San Francisco, CA — Nearly a third of all Americans have some kind of allergy. Chart Yu figured there had to be a way to help Americans breathe easier, so he created Gazoontite, a consumer-friendly retail store devoted to allergy products.

In 1997, Yu voluntarily gave up his management position at Clorox to become a sales clerk at Crate & Barrel—a daring move that gave him valuable retail experience at 15 percent of his previous salary. He easily could have spent the next several decades trying to learn all the other aspects of running a successful startup business. Instead, he began seeking out resources to help him formulate a realistic business plan. A visit to the San Francisco office of the Small Business Administration led him to the local chapter of SCORE.

"SCORE helped me understand the big picture—addressing consumer needs and developing a strategy for meeting them," Yu says. "We covered everything from the first small steps to the long term moves that would sustain my company's growth."

Yu's first Gazoontite store opened on San Francisco's upscale Union Street in April 1999. A month later, gazoontite.com debuted in cyberspace. Both were immediate hits for allergy sufferers and their families. Yu's idea also sparked interest in the financial community, attracting over $30 million of venture capital financing that has allowed Gazoontite to open stores in New York, Chicago, and Costa Mesa, California.

Help for Freon Sniffer

Townsend, VT — The Instrument Division of Janos Technology developed a significant product that has the ability to detect freon-based refrigerants. U.S. and import auto manufacturers are considering whether to offer the tool as "mandated" or "optional" tool to dealers. Specifically, Ford and GM are looking to this device to comply with clean-air standards to refrigerant recycling. The company received a $600,000 guarantee loan through the Department of Agriculture Rural Business Services.

The company continues to be successful, and currently provides 77 jobs for its community. Funding will be used for company expansion and is expected to save the existing 77 jobs while providing 10 new jobs.

Fiberglass Auto Parts

Grand Ledge, MI — E-T-M Enterprises manufactures reinforced fiberglass parts for truck, automotive, and recreational vehicle manufacturers. A guaranteed loan from the Department of Agriculture enabled the company to expand its manufacturing plant. The project saved 330 jobs currently provided by the company and will create an additional 230 jobs.

Wood Products

Medford, OR — Southern Oregon Regional Development Inc. is in the Pacific Northwest Economic Adjustment Initiative (PNWEAI) and funds are from the PNWEAI reserve. Preference was extended to businesses that create or retain industrial production of wood products. Southern Oregon Regional Economic Development, Inc. (SO-REDI), estimates that by targeting a maximum of $20,000 per job created or saved, the $1,500,000 IRP loan will create or save at least 50 jobs in the fund's first round of loans for the communities of this two-county area. SO-REDI has initially identified 28 potential small businesses that could benefit from the IRP funds. IRP credit needs for these businesses total approximately $2,000,000.

Seed Conditioning

West Lebanon, IN — Hubner Industries purchased a seed conditioning plant. The company purchases raw seed corn and soybeans to condition, packages and stores in a warehouse, and distributes to wholesalers and retailers. They received funding of $2,400,000 through the Department of Agriculture Rural Business Service Loan Guarantee Program. They will export some seed to Italy, France, and Spain. The funding resulted in the creation of 24 new jobs.

Zero-Cost Consultant Spots Problem

Vienna, VA — This couple bought a five-year-old quick-print shop with four employees. Within a year they ran into many problems. Primarily, they were unable to do more than break even. Somebody introduced them to a management consultant who charged them $80 for the first session. As the shop owners anticipated a long consulting relationship at considerable costs, a friend told them about the Washington area Service Corps of Retired Executives (SCORE) office. An experienced management expert from SCORE quickly pointed to the problem: employee inefficiency. It was a tough decision, but one man was laid off and a profit leak in the business was immediately plugged. "Five out of six small businesses fail during the first two years," said the counselor, "due firstly to poor management, and secondly to lack of adequate financing."

Seven Percent Interest Reduction

Valparaiso, IN — After 22 years as an employee in the food industry, this man decided to go into the wholesale meat packing business with his three sons. They obtained financing through the SBA but at high rates existing at that time—15½ percent. Within a few months it became clear that the business could not take off as quickly as anticipated, and that the onerous financing terms were making survival impossible. An old friend who was now a counselor with the nearby SCORE office went to bat for the new entrepreneur and arranged with the SBA rescheduled repayment at 81/2 percent. Now, nearly seven years later, the business is prospering and its products can be found from Detroit to Chicago.

SCORE Team Helps Float Business to Success

Boise, ID — A vacation in the Idaho River country led San Francisco businessman, D.T., into a partnership with a local river raft builder. At first, the company's quality products enabled it to grow from $250,000 to $750,000 annual gross. However, such rapid expansion brought its problems, namely purchasing, scheduling, inventory control, production snafus and managing employees, which had grown from three to eleven people. A call to the local SBA office got them in touch with a retired Boise Cascade executive who was now a volunteer SCORE counselor. With his continued help and another experienced volunteer, new production schedules were worked out and quality products restored. The SCORE counselors have become an integral pan of the firm's team and at no cost to the company. This was truly free help from Uncle Sam!

Cemetery Saved from Going Under

Albert Lea, MN — Privately-owned and -operated cemeteries can be big business, but like all enterprises, they are subject to the risks and frailties of private enterprise. The local burial facility had been a family-owned business until it suffered a number of acquisitions by absentee owners. Advance payments for graves and a mausoleum were absconded and the property was embroiled in litigation and bad public relations. While the state filed charges against the latest owners, investors in the cemetery banded together and formed a cooperative association, obtained the court's approval to try and save the company, and brought in a SCORE team from nearby Minneapolis to offer a revival plan. More than 500 lot owners were located, brought together, and offered the SCORE reorganization plan. The latter hands-on assistance and the establishment of a volunteer board of directors brought the nearly defunct cemetery back to life again.

5

Community Taken by Storm after Tornado

Council Bluffs, IA — A tornado caused $30,000,000 worth of damage and the local mayor called in the local SCORE chapter to get the town back into business. Within six days, 18 members met to map out a rescue plan. One hundred thirty-four businesses were damaged; $4,500,000 was needed; 105 workers were put back to production. SCORE assisted in getting disaster loans and federal retraining programs, becoming an arm of the small municipal staff and helping 131 businesses to open again.

Incubator Community Breeds Small Business Success

Golden, CO — The Business and Innovation Center is called an incubator because it "hatches" fledgling businesses into full-blown enterprises. It has, on an average, 14 tenants in its 8,500 square feet of space at the Denver West Office Park. A Small Business Development Center (SBDC) is also located here as well as a nearby SCORE office, whose members volunteer their time to help new, small businesses become successful. Partial support comes from private industry through corporate membership. Subsidies usually operate for the first three years of the small businesses accepted into the incubator program. The incubators are expected to grow into self-sufficiency within that time and "graduate" into outside facilities. Most incubator facilities are affiliated with universities, where professional and academic personnel are available to assist in guidance and advisory capacities. The National Business Incubation Association is located at 20 East Circle Drive, Suite 190, Athens, Ohio, 45701. Phone is (740) 593-4331.

Sweet on Sourdough

San Luis Obispo, CA — A couple who loved San Francisco sourdough bread decided that the area was ripe for a hometown bakery that furnished locals with the Golden Bay's famed specialty. They leased a 2500 sq. ft. building, obtained two small loans from a lender who was backed by SBA guaranties, hired one expert employee, lined up two outlets, and began producing 150 one-pound loaves each night. It took but three weeks to increase production, due to word-of-mouth demand. Next, the company expanded into a new 18,000 sq. ft. building and increased its market into much of Southern California. Sales rose to $3,000,000 due to the right amount of dough—from San Francisco and the SBA.

Gourmet Cookie Company Kneads Way to Wealth

New York City — The Big Apple appears to be a tough orchard in which to grow a new company. However, a California woman transplanted to New York City opened her own deluxe cookie company after six years of work apprenticeship at a leading hotel. A friend recommended the local SCORE chapter as a counseling resource, and she attended a pre-business workshop. One of the counselors helped her in the preparation of a business plan. The latter identified competition, needed production levels for desired cash flow, location, and personnel requirements. Her initial factory was in a wholesale bakery. She attended local gift shows and utilized trade publications for publicity and small ads. The next year she opened a trial retail shop and moved into her own baking facility. The assigned SCORE counselor was with her every step of the way and the combined efforts have paid dividends.

Business Higher Than a Kite

San Diego, CA — Two brothers who as boys loved flying kites, realized their young dreams by going into the manufacturing of scientifically designed kites. Of course, in the growing-up process, one of the brothers became an aeronautical engineer with an MBA from USC, while the other became an engineer-designer. A "big brother" was added when the local SCORE office was approached for some free business assistance to the new company, which was located in a garage. The SCORE counselor, with experience in export, advised them to look into foreign trade. A trip to Japan resulted in a working relationship with the huge Sony Corporation. The business is still a family affair (mother is the number one helper) and is prospering. Says one of the brother partners, "I never thought we'd get in so far, so fast."

SBA Deposits $450,000 in Schnitzel Bank

Shepherdstown, WV — Running a successful restaurant is the dream of thousands of entrepreneurs. Love does indeed go through the stomach. However, a restaurant can also become an investor's nightmare. The Bavarian Inn, run by experienced restaurateurs from Munich, Germany, Erwin and Carol Asam, is a shining exception of a dream come true. Local banks put together $750,000 to help the business expand, and the SBA, approached by the banks, added another $450,000 the following year. This infusion of capital enabled the inn to increase its volume from $600,000 to $1,000,000. Now sales are in excess of $3,000,000 and nearly a hundred people find employment here. Superior food and accommodations, backed by real expertise and financial security enabled this very tricky business to become an annual award winner.

Hazardous Waste Companies Have Rosy Opportunities

Miami, FL — One of the nation's pioneers in hazardous waste management, control, and disposal is Enviropact, Inc. They started with more foresight than experience and grew in importance and size until the SBA guaranteed a bank loan of $430,000 to expand the operation. The company paid it back in less than four years. Revenue originally was less than $3,000,000. It has since skyrocketed to more than $30,000,000 with a commensurate growth in employees. Opportunities in the environment are prolific. EPA, SBA, and virtually every government agency have financial aid programs for the alert entrepreneur in this field.

Hispanic Firm Plays Winning Ball with SBA

Morton, TX — Ben Ansolabehere (he's of Basque origin) runs a company called Great Western Meat Company. It employs about 300 people, mostly Mexican-Americans, and does around $40,000,000 in annual business. When Ben first started, he got a boost from the SBA with a $300,000 loan, supplemented since then with $500,000. The investment was worth it and loans have been repaid. Great Western now exports $36,000,000 of horse meat to France, sells equine organs to pharmaceutical companies for serum production, and the horse hides to baseball manufacturers. In fact, 40 percent of America's baseballs are covered with leather produced in Morton, Texas. It's been a win-win game for all sides.

Baby Superstore ·

Greenville, SC — Twenty years ago Jack Tate graduated from Harvard as a young lawyer. Two years later, while his wife, Ginny, was raising their baby, lawyer Tate changed law books for diapers and opened a large baby store. The very first year, a combination of timing, good research, and hard work helped the Tates reach a volume of $500,000. Within eight years, expansion of the business, now called Baby Superstore, enabled the SBA to come up with an expansion loan of $460,000. Today the firm has over two dozen franchise stores, annual sales of $27,000,000, and employs over 350 people in stores averaging 20,000 sq. ft. each. Success came before the money, but the SBA helped to lubricate the company's growth at the right time.

Hot Dog! Maine's Small Business Person of the Year

Portland, ME — H. Allen Ryan worked for a hot dog and luncheon meat producer in the state of Maine. With the SBA's help he transformed it into a dynamo, offering 4,000 different food and non-food items to 1,400 restaurants, schools, and hospitals. "The local bank insisted on an SBA guarantee as part of their commitment, meaning that without SBA's help the whole deal was likely to die," disclosed Ryan. "I found SBA to be detailed, professional, and very helpful during the negotiations for the guarantee. They asked tough questions as they sought to balance the interests of the taxpayer and their responsibility to assist small companies. In the end, they saved our deal. Without SBA's help, I might not own our growing business today."

Federal Express: SBA Was There at the Creation

Federal Express vice president Fred Smith, whose family founded Dixie Greyhound, started his air package delivery service in Memphis, Tennessee.

Undercapitalized and overreaching, the company had lost close to $7,000,000 in the first few months. There was no partial bail-out possible—Smith determined he needed no less than $24,500,000 of investment capital (to be matched by banks) in order to service the dozens of cities that would make the new delivery concept both profitable and efficient. Meanwhile, as one report put it, "the company was being held together with bailing wire."

SBA's Small Business Investment Companies (SBICs) supplied 20 percent or roughly $5,000,000 of financing needed by Federal Express when the young firm was in its critical start-up years.

Some 51,000 people are working at Federal Express (up from only 518 at the time of SBA's involvement). The $3,000,000,000 company created a new concept in hard copy delivery and a whole industry of competitors as well.

From A $75 Parking Lot Striper Machine to Riches

Steven Neighbors of Boise, Idaho, swept parking lots as a schoolboy. He noticed that many lots needed fresh stripes to guide drivers into parking spaces. When the opportunity to buy a $75 striping machine came along, he took it.

"I had a dream to start a road-striping business and was not taken seriously by anyone but the SBA. Their personnel listened seriously to a kid who looked fifteen, and set in motion for him to be trained to consider market, project goals, cash flow, etc. In essence, the Small Business Administration, with the commitment of a direct loan of $10,000 and an investment of time, created a small businessman."

The investment of time was provided chiefly by SBA's SCORE counselor Jim Cheatham, a retired engineer, and Nancy Guiles, a loan officer, in the Boise district office. The result is business history. Neighbors' company, Eterna-Line Corp., was listed among Inc. magazine's 500 fastest-growing private companies for several years. Annual sales went from $5,000 at the time of the SBA loan to $10,000,000 today. Currently there are 200 employees.

Canvas Tarps Made in a Basement

He invented a beltless tarp that rolls automatically over a truck full of grain. His hardwood veneers adorn many renovated homes across the land. But what makes Ed Shorma most happy is that there are at least fifteen nationalities among his 220 employees at Wahpeton Canvas in North Dakota.

You wouldn't expect Malaysians and Indonesians to work in 30°-below-zero weather, or what Northerners call white-out storms. But Shorma has sponsored dozens of refugees from many lands, and has gone one step further—he's given them jobs.

Up-from-the-bootstraps stories don't involve SBA—that's the conventional misconception. After an unsuccessful stint at farming and a term in the state legislature, Shorma wanted to go full tilt with canvas-making. To effect a move from a basement to a downtown space, SBA loaned Shorma $75,000. The extra space was put to immediate use manufacturing original equipment seats for Canadian farm equipment makers—helping the trade balance in the days when it wasn't so unbalanced.

At the time of SBA's first loan, Wahpeton Canvas had gross annual sales of $147,000 and seventeen employees. Today the firm sells

The Pretty Puny Pickle Packer

Like relish on your hot dog? Have a yen for sweet (or dill) pickles? Chances are, sometime in the past thirty years, most Americans have enjoyed a product of Atkins Pickle Company of Atkins, Arkansas. Think of the Ozarks the next time you taste a good, long, green pickle. And think of the SBA—without it, Atkins would have remained a small, unknown pickle packer.

The pickle company received a $350,000 SBA loan when it had less than $1,000,000 in annual sales and 100 employees. Today Atkins Pickle has $20,000,000 in yearly sales and 400 employees.

Fishing Boat Success

Ever heard of a startup fishing boat? It happens. With a loan of $500,000, SBA helped launch the Huntress II and its captain, Richard Goodwin, into the fishing waters off the coast of Rhode Island. According to James Hague, district director in the Providence office, "Our major consideration in approving the SBA portion of this loan was that under-utilized species such as mackerel, hake, herring, and scup, not widely consumed in the United States, would be processed and exported to foreign markets such as Japan, Spain, and other European countries."

The Huntress II employs forty workers, and annual sales in the first year were $2,400,000, substantially exceeding expectations. Sales doubled in the second year. Huntress, Inc. recently purchased a second ship for $1,200,000, which will employ up to fifteen new workers.

"The fishing industry in Rhode Island has always been a risky business," said Buddy Violet of Ocean State Business Development Authority (OSBDA). "But these new boats are to fishing what Babe Ruth was to baseball. Phenomenal!" Violet noted that SBA was a crucial partner in the project. The state of

Rhode Island "could not have gone anywhere else to cinch the deal but the SBA," he said.

Government at Apple's Core

An SBA-backed Small Business Investment Company (SBIC) provided $504,000 in equity financing to Steve Jobs and Steve Wozniak, founders of Apple Computer. The company made $42,000 in profit that year. Only fifteen years later, Apple Computer enjoyed annual sales of $6,300,000,000 and employed 10,000 people.

Mexican Restaurant Big Hit

Who said SBA won't back a startup restaurant?

Mariano Martinez, Jr. gathered every resource he could to start a restaurant in Dallas' Old Town Shopping Center. He had $5,000 of his own money, and he borrowed $5,000 from his father, $5,000 from a friend, and $51,000 from SBA. By year's end, Martinez had 60 employees and annual sales of $350,000.

Over the next twelve years, Martinez opened a second restaurant in Arlington, Texas, with SBA help ($390,000 loan), and another in Dallas with a $243,000 loan.

Today, employment at the firm has increased to 200, and annual sales exceed $3,000,000. The original loan is paid off, while the others remain current.

Plenty of Bread in the U.S.

Samir Saleh fled Lebanon when civil war broke out. He came to the U.S. and with his uncle's help started a bakery.

Uncle Moussa also "was aware of the resources of SBA," according to Samir. At first there was a pessimistic assessment by a SCORE counselor and the internationally known baking consultant Frank Dadon. But soon, Fred Fried, a retired Westinghouse financial supervisor and SCORE counselor, was giving the Salehs help with business planning and accounting. Along the way, two SBA loans gave the Salehs a boost. A $100,000 loan covered new machinery and a small debt to a credit union. Three years later, an additional loan of $178,000 helped the bakery expand to four times its original size.

"For people in our situation, SBA's assistance is the best thing that ever existed," said a grateful Samir. "Only in America could three young immigrant boys with little previous business experience come so far in ten short years."

SCORE Classes in an Indiana Prison

Richard Dasse of the Northwest Indiana Chapter of the Service Corps of Retired Executives (SCORE) recalls when he and his SCORE associate began providing management training seminars in a most unusual place—an Indiana prison. "Afraid? You bet we were. We feared for our safety, and we really wondered if anyone would be interested."

Now, after three years of providing assistance at the Westville Correctional Center, Dasse acknowledges, "This is not exactly a Sunday School atmosphere," but adds: "We're tremendously impressed. The interest is great, and we've encountered some brilliant individuals."

The courses offered at Westville, a medium-security institution located about an hour's drive from Chicago, are similar to those a small business person might find "on the outside"—a pre-business workshop, one on small business management, another on challenges specific to small business, and another on small business sales.

Intel — A Giant in Byte-Size Chips

It's the eighth largest manufacturer of semiconductors in the world (and one of only three American companies in the top ten). It's responsible for two of the major postwar innovations in micro-electronics that have made today's electronic age possible—large-scale integrated (LSI) memory and the microprocessor. Its computer chips, software, and minicomputers drive everything from digital gasoline pumps to scanner cash registers in supermarkets.

It's Intel. And when it was a one-year-old baby company, with 218 employees and $565,874 in sales, it received SBA-backed Small Business Investment Company equity of $299,390. Today, Intel has 19,200 employees and annual sales of $1,900,000,000. It has often approached and even surpassed achievements of rivals Motorola and Texas Instruments—two corporate giants when Intel was a startup small business.

A large percentage of Intel's total revenues come from abroad, making the company one of the top fifty U.S.-based manufacturing exporters. Who ever thought that a well placed bit of SBA-backed equity twenty years ago would be a key force in helping to fight our trade deficit?

Hardware Store in Wyoming

The number one store in the 1,500-store coast-to-coast chain of hardware stores rests in the mountain town of Casper, Wyoming. Owner Ed Bratt claims, "If it hadn't been for the SBA loan, I doubt we'd have even got off the ground."

When Ed and Joyce Bratt tried to find funds to start a retail hardware store, banks shut them out. But by year's end, SBA came to the rescue with a startup guaranteed loan of $175,000. "On opening day we sold twelve percent of our inventory," Ed relates.

No surprise that the loan was paid off in three years. With ten employees then, the Bratts now employ 39; their annual sales volume is $3,000,000.

Ice Cream Fails to Melt

Life with the 140-year-old Applegate Farm in Montclair, New Jersey, was anything but bright for Betty Vhay. Since purchasing the dairy farm, Vhay had endured more than the usual set of hard knocks. Money was chronically low; neighbors brought a lawsuit against the farm over "loud" machinery that was making ice cream; she went through a bitter divorce. It seemed to her at times that the circumstances of the farm's purchase were an ill omen. After losing an unborn child in an auto accident, she had taken $100,000 in settlement money to stake her future on Applegate Farm.

Alone, and with two children to support, Vhay pulled out all stops in the search for money for the ice cream operation. Bank after bank turned her down as a credit risk. Then the Money Store Investment Corporation took a chance on Vhay and provided her with an SBA-guaranteed loan of $170,000. For the first time, she had working capital, was sole owner, and recorded her first profit.

At first Vhay employed 10; today she employs 52, most of whom are teenagers outfitted with their first job as ice cream barflies. Annual sales grew to $700,000 from $420,000 in six years.

Black Ex-Marine and Jewish Female Consultant Create United Nations Drilling Company

A Black man and a Jewish woman—not your usual business team in critical pre-construction testing! It happened in the Bronx.

In a highly-specialized field hardly open to minorities and women, Garrett W. Brown, a Vietnam veteran, and Honie Ann Peacock, a consultant in employee relations, drill for "dirt" samples in the chasms of the Big Apple as Python Drilling and Testing.

Their first year was not a good one for construction. There were nights without dinner and weeks when payroll was met on a credit card. Peacock, a single parent, took two outside jobs and worked full-time without pay to help get the fledgling company off the ground. Brown, an ex-Marine sergeant who specialized in heavy construction equipment and diesel engines, brought 20 years of experience in the construction industry to the company. He designed and built their first drill rig in his living room.

Peacock wrote the loan proposal and marketing plan that enabled the company to receive a $50,000 direct loan from SBA, which bought them their first big drill rig and truck. Today their 16-person crew has been trained completely from within and represents a virtual "United Nations," including Blacks, Filipinos, Hispanics, Irish, and Finns, both male and female.

Though it has been an uphill struggle to gain the confidence of their numerous clients, Brown and Peacock maintain a positive attitude. And why not? From the time of SBA's loan, annual sales have grown from $30,000 to over $1,000,000.

Doughnut-Making Machine Export Success

Li'l Orbits, a Minneapolis manufacturer of a miniature doughnut-making machine and doughnut mix, turned to the Department of Commerce for export assistance. The Department provided publicity with their New Product Information Service (NPIS) along with a description in *Commercial News* magazine, both distributed widely abroad. The products were also exhibited at a fast food exhibition in Paris, France.

"It looks like we're in the export business to stay," reports Li'l Orbits president Ed Anderson. "Results to date are gratifying. Worldwide publicity through this program has resulted in sales of the machine to firms in Japan, Thailand, Germany, and the West Indies." These efforts resulted in $575,000 in sales. Inquiries from Jamaica, the Philippines, Singapore, Norway, Korea, and Denmark are expected to yield further sales.

Rebuilt Transmissions and Engines

Tracom, Inc., a small Fort Worth company, rebuilds automotive transmissions and engines. The Department of Commerce consulted with them about the potential for exporting, identified the appropriate foreign firms, and helped prepare a sales letter.

Another sale was to an Australian distributor for $470,000!

Sales increased from $250,000 a year to $2,500,000. Currently they sell to many foreign markets including the United Kingdom, Kuwait, and New Zealand.

Wholesale Computer Supplies

Digital Storage International, a company with six employees, handles magnetic media such as diskettes, tapes, and data cartridges in Columbus, Ohio. A slow domestic market compelled them to look elsewhere. The Department of Commerce's Agent Distributor Service (ADS) helped locate overseas representatives. The Cincinnati DOC office also provided export counseling. This help led to expansion into 28 countries.

Department of Energy Helps Software Firm

The Department of Energy funds projects under its Small Business Innovation Research (SBIR) program. It helped Emerson and Stem Associates, a small San Diego firm, develop software for elementary and junior high students using Apple computers. They then negotiated a licensing agreement with a major software publisher for production and distribution.

Department of Health Helps Launch Firm

Data Sciences had two employees and a good idea. They wanted to develop devices to help gather information for pharmaceutical firms from experiments via an implantable transmitter that monitors various body functions. They presented the idea to the Department of Health and Human Services, and received financial backing.

As a result of this help, the firm has grown to 12 persons and is selling about $20,000 worth of devices per month.

Department of Defense Funds Research

Ultramet, a Pacoima, California, firm, had an idea for a coating for rocket engines that won't corrode and is tolerant of high temperatures. The DOD's Small Business Innovation Research program provided funds to develop it. Ultramet is now selling this product to major aerospace companies.

National Science Foundation Helps Company Fight Pollution

Tracer Technologies, located in Newton, Maine, wanted to build an anti-pollution device. Funds from National Science Foundation through its Small Business Innovation Research program enabled them to do that. They came up with a gadget that can separate chlorinated hydrocarbons so that they can be burned in ordinary furnaces. A service business was launched as a result.

Pizza Analysis

The owner of a pizza shop was having problems with pizza consistency, and productivity. The Commerce Productivity Center sent information on statistical process control, cause and effect diagramming, and other techniques so he could monitor and analyze the process of preparing pizza, and determine the probable causes of the consistency problem. The CPC also provided him with information on providing quality service to the customer, measuring productivity, and how to study and improve workflow and equipment location. Japanese housekeeping "Five S" principles were instigated:

- Sort out the clutter
- Set things in order and standardize
- Shine equipment, tools, and workplace
- Share information, no searching
- Stick to the rules
- Other principles he learned were:
- Clutter hides problems
- Storage spaces should be self-regulating through visual controls
- Cleaning equipment is a form of inspection
- Make information easily accessible; for example, place operating procedures on machines

Cultural Help

The American manager of a small West Coast electronics firm was having problems managing the engineers of Singapore and American-Chinese origin. The Commerce Productivity Center sent data on the work-related values, attitudes, and habits of these ethnic groups, which are different than those of American workers. The manager studied the data and instituted more appropriate policies. The result: increased productivity.

The Effect of Cold on Workers

A Northeast construction contractor's job was delayed by legal problems. Outdoor construction was going to have to be done in winter instead of in warmer weather, as had been planned. The owner wanted to know how much productivity would decline because of cold, inclement weather so he could adjust his prices. The Commerce Productivity Center located and sent formulas and information on how construction productivity is affected at different temperatures.

The Effect of Lighting

A floor plan for remodeling some offices at a company had been developed. The plan called for every worker to have a window in his office. The boss didn't think this was a good idea. The remodeling planners called to find out if employees with windows in their offices are more productive. The Commerce Productivity Center researched the problem and offered the findings. Workers with windows are happier, but not necessarily more productive. The real issue is proper lighting. Windows and sunlight aren't necessarily appropriate. The best lighting is that which is designed for the particular tasks being performed; proper lighting improves performance. And lighting can be designed for energy efficiency and save money.

The Effect of Nightshift

A contractor was remodeling an office building's interior during the daytime. The remodeling made so much noise that the building's occupants couldn't get any work done. The occupants got a court injunction forcing the contractor to do the work at night.

When the night work started, the productivity of the contractor's workforce dropped dramatically. The contractor called for help; the Commerce Productivity Center researched the problem and found the probable cause.

People have an internal biological clock set by routine. Your body tells you when to wake up, when to eat, and when to go to sleep. When the workers suddenly shifted to night work, their biological clocks were disrupted. It produced a jet-lag-type effect.

Studies show that an individual's productivity can decline until the biological clock adjusts to the new routine. There was a stress-producing disruption in the workers' routines and schedules.

Saving Money on Wine

A small winery was losing money and needed to cut its costs. The winery had also been hiring full-time employees for jobs that took less than full time. The Commerce Productivity Center provided information on how to study the production process to identify waste in areas such as transportation, work in process, machine setup, non-value adding activities, storage, defects, et al., and on developing multi-skilled, multi-functional workers.

Good Advice at the Last Minute

The International Operations Group helps small businesses with their uncertainties concerning foreign clients. For example:

The president of a small consulting company heard that a potential Japanese client was coming to town the next day, on extremely short notice, and would be available for meetings. The International Operations Group helped the company locate information about the company, its products, and recent company activities, so that the consultant made a favorable impression and acquired the Japanese firm as a client.

Ever Been Buried by Your Work?

A rapid transit system contractor was involved in trenching and excavating and asked for help in protecting his workers. A Department of Labor consultant in the Occupational Safety and Health Administration (OSHA) was called for a confidential, risk-free evaluation (i.e., the consultant would not issue any citations for violations of state or federal safety standards). The consultant arrived the day after a heavy rain and found some workers in a twelve-foot deep trench that was not shored nor sloped. He advised immediate evacuation; the supervisor ordered all workers out of the trench. Ten minutes later the sides of the trench gave way. The workers would have been buried. The consultant showed the contractor a six-step plan to resume work safely.

The Government Cures Headaches

Workers at a small auto parts custom electroplating shop were having headaches. A gas-fired hot-water boiler had recently been installed. An OSHA consultant analyzed the problem: Carbon monoxide from the boiler was coming into the building because there was no vent to bring fresh air to the boiler, and, the exhaust fans, instead of helping, were making the problem worse. The employer, with the consultant's help, was able to fix the problem easily.

Meat Packer Gets Solution to Hazard Problem

A meat packer's employees worked on a slippery platform 10 feet above a concrete floor. The employees stood on the edge, working with power tools on carcasses suspended from a moving conveyor.

The platform was slippery with animal fat. Guardrails could not be used since they would inhibit the conveyor. The employer contacted other meat packers and found that none had a solution.

An OSHA consultant gave a free, confidential, no-hassle safety survey. He recommended the employees wear a body belt with a lanyard attached by a sliding ring to an overhead rail. The employees thought they wouldn't like it, but after trying it found it convenient and comfortable, and it didn't slow them up.

Census Data Helps Sales

A manufacturer of corrugated boxes contacted the U.S. Census Bureau to help him analyze his sales in the state of Arizona. At the time, he was selling primarily to food packaging companies. Using census data, he found the market potential was 15 times larger than he was experiencing. Lumber, pottery, and glass industries in Arizona also needed his products and he successfully marketed to these previously unidentified customers.

A manufacturer of products for dairy farms used census data to locate counties with large numbers of dairy farms. By next determining which were the most prosperous, he was able to optimize his marketing efforts.

Government Publication Brings $2,500,000 in Sales

Barrier Industries of Baton Rouge, Louisiana, manufactures an insecticidal paint called "Bug-X." They approached the Department of Commerce, who suggested worldwide exposure in the U.S. Government publication *Commercial News USA*. Information on "Bug-X" resulted in $2,500,000 in sales. The firm has signed six overseas agents and reports another eighteen under negotiation.

Teenage Landscape Entrepreneur

A Pennsylvania teenager applied for and received a Department of Agriculture Youth Project Loan to start a landscaping business. He purchased all of the necessary equipment and operated the business for three years before moving on to bigger things.

Grant for Solar-Powered Outhouse

A Missouri inventor applied for and received a grant to research and construct a solar-energized outhouse. The Above Ground Aerobic and Solar-Assisted Composting Toilet uses solar energy to decompose waste.

SCORE Helps Two Young Ladies Launch Butcher Shop

An old-fashioned butcher shop where you can buy ready-cut and portioned meats, but also obtain cut-to-order steaks and roasts, is the unusual business of a pair of young women from Ohio. The father of one has a meat market in another area and he taught his daughter the business. With the help of a knowledgeable SCORE counselor they were able to draft a credible business plan and obtain an SBA-guaranteed loan of $150,000. The money advanced to the two entrepreneurs was used to purchase display cases, a walk-in freezer, smokehouse, and double oven. With continued help from SCORE counselors, lots of enthusiasm and hard work, the two women recreated a business that had been a vanishing breed—and customers have been coming from near and far because they learned that the shop's products were truly a cut above.

SCORE Helps Prevent Loss of Lifetime Savings

This is a non-success story and it could apply to any business anywhere. This one comes from San Diego where a man who had been pensioned from a large company had a bundle of cash to invest. He liked the liquor business because of its quick turnover, constant business, and easy-to-handle merchandise. A business broker offered him two stores on the market for $300,000. Fortunately, even though he had his mind pretty well made up to buy them, he followed a friend's advice and contacted the local SCORE office.

A counselor with many years of liquor store experience did his own investigation of the stores—checking inventory, merchandise, traffic flow, competition, service handling, pricing—and then recommended against the acquisition. It was $100,000 overpriced. The locations were weak. The competition from big chains and discount stores was overwhelming. Despite his enthusiasm, the would-be entrepreneur finally realized the SCORE counselor's wisdom and withdrew his offer — possibly saving his lifetime assets before, like alcohol, they could evaporate.

SCORE Doubles Jewelry Designer's Business

A jewelry designer in Seattle happened to see a story on SCORE in her local newspaper. It stimulated her to seek free counseling and explore her desire to go into a retail business. First off, the counselor guided her in executing a viable business plan, then advised her on seeking and securing a good location.

A seven-step plan was developed under which she doubled her business after the first year. The counselor still helps out after four years, including proposing a "Men's Night" promotion before Christmas, which turned out to be the year's most productive sales event.

Rags to Riches for Fashion Designer

In Massachusetts, a young African-American mother, divorced, with two children, and struggling along on sheer guts and hard work, heard about SCORE and requested an appointment. The assigned counselor evaluated her talent and enthusiasm accurately.

Her unique use of knit fabrics and design combined with her capability and vitality led to creating a media event around her. A publicity campaign was planned that attracted a number of local notables and generated considerable press coverage.

A well-executed projection and business plan enabled her to get an SBA-guaranteed loan that allowed for the addition of several sewing machines and more workers. Currently, she heads her own design studio, producing fashions under her own label, and has gone national with her line. She was selected as "Woman of the Year" in New England.

Day Care Center — Just Kid Stuff to SCORE

Reading in the papers that day care centers are one of the most needed and hottest enterprises, a man-and-wife team of corporate executives saw an opportunity to go into business for themselves. They decided to start an upscale, after-school, youth-sitting service for latchkey kids in their Connecticut community.

The local SCORE counselors helped them set up a proper business plan and, to conserve limited capital, suggested a direct mail campaign to specific, higher income neighborhoods. Another counselor suggested publicity for the unique venture that was quite successful.

They opened "Kidstop" with seven young customers. Within the year the business had expanded to 64. "The SCORE counselors were a dramatic help to us," said the owners. "We're going to continue using and benefiting from their expertise."

Ornamental Plant Business Blooms Overseas

A large grower of ornamental plants in Florida was trying to sell his plants overseas where a potentially uncrowded and lucrative market awaited him. However, he found that it took more plants to fill a traditional container than he could produce, and more expertise and money than he could manage. So he explored the idea with other growers throughout the state. The result was a cooperative association of growers.

They hired a coordinator-promoter familiar with marketing in Holland and Western Europe. During their first year, the cooperative group sold $2,000,000 worth of plants.

The best was yet to come, however. A SCORE counselor helped reorganize the co-op and initiate a newsletter and promotion material to use at European trade fairs. In 1986, export volume

29

increased six times to $12,000,000. It's currently $18,000,000 and growing.

Inventor Gets Help from the Department of Energy

A Detroit, Michigan, inventor developed a system that senses knocking in an automobile engine and controls the spark timing in individual cylinders. The idea was submitted to the Office of Energy-Related Inventions run by the National Institute of Standards and Technology (formerly National Bureau of Standards).

The invention got a favorable review and the government assisted him in bringing it to market. The inventor licensed his system to Ford Motor Company in exchange for royalties.

The Fastest-Growing Hispanic Firm in Arizona

Phoenix, AZ — Roberto Ruiz's Maya Construction is also the tenth fastest-growing Hispanic firm in the nation. With the SBA's help, sales went from $1,700 a year in 1978 to $23,000,000 in ten years. Ruiz has built everything from schools at Fort Huachuca to a water distribution system (including drinking fountains) for the National Park Service in the Grand Canyon. Maya has built private and state building, roadway, and underground water and sewer projects, as well. Seeing himself "as a coach, not a captain" of his company, Ruiz likes to act "as a cheering section for employees, to tell them when they're on target and guide them when they're not." Twice a year, he and his top managers take a two-day retreat to plot Maya's business future.

Ruiz has garnered many accolades, including Arizona Small Business Person of the Year and National Minority Contractor of the Year. SBA likes to think of itself as a cheering section for this intrepid Mexican-American.

Long-Term Relationships with SCORE

Supermarkets are admittedly one of the toughest businesses next to running a restaurant. This Indiana family supermarket has had the longest counseling arrangement of any business in the U.S. — and all with the local SCORE counselors. For sixteen years one or several members of the Service Corps of Retired Executives have advised them.

Ownership is now in its second generation. Ironically, the family-owned business was encouraged to take over the vacant premises of a former Kroger supermarket that had a well-established location.

SCORE counseled budgeting, financial planning, quality assurance, promotion, and the kind of public relations that chain stores could not provide. They helped the family to get into computerization as well as guide them into each step of planned expansions.

Fired Man Builds Uniform Chain

"I was fired into greatness," quips Harvey Hafetz of his dismissal from a job as a sales representative for a cosmetics distributor. Of course, that's today — then it was a painful experience. Harvey's wife, Zena, had decided just that year to leave her job as an elementary school teacher and try another challenge. The couple purchased a small uniform shop in Reading, Pennsylvania, as an investment and to give Zena part-time on-the-job training for a new career. But when Harvey lost his job, he joined his wife at the little store. Z&H Uniforms was born.

Today, the company has twenty retail stores, mostly in shopping malls, and eleven leased departments catering primarily to health care professionals. A contract sales department furnishes executive-type apparel, hospitality, food service, and industrial-type clothing to industry.

Z&H added ten stores after acquiring a Philadelphia-based competitor's stores with the help of a $600,000 SBA-guaranteed $12,000,000 worth of goods a year, and has 220 employees. Not a bad return on investment! loan from Meridian Bank. The firm had 75 employees then: only three years later, it has 170. Annual sales volume has doubled in that time, from $3,500,000 to $7,000,000.

Thermal Bags by Ingrid

A 12-employee, Des Plaines, Illinois, firm makes insulated bags for catering and food delivery. In five years the firm has gone from zero to approximately $900,000 in sales. Ingrid exhibited at a trade show attended by foreign firms but their orders were too large for her to fulfill.

She contacted the Commerce Department's International Trade Administration and described her problem. They arranged for her to attend an export-financing seminar.

"Now we know how to do it," Ingrid says. "We couldn't have done it without the guidance we received from the Commerce Department."

They now export to England, Norway, Australia, Sweden, the Netherlands, Spain, France, Mexico, and Panama.

CHAPTER 2

Startups on a Shoestring

You might need less money from Uncle Sam—or any other lender—than you think. One thing about borrowing money from either source: you have to expect to pay it back, usually with interest. So, if you can figure out a way of doing with less money (without, of course, jeopardizing your progress and operation), then why not check it out?

More than a century ago, many famous, present-day companies started on the proverbial shoestring. Of course, these are the survivors among many who have disappeared from view. Still, they show some common characteristics that hold as true today as they did then: the need for the product or service in the marketplace, a quality product or service, hard work, measured growth, patience and persistence in balanced measure.

Famous Companies That Began on a Shoestring

Pittsburgh, PA, 1875—H. J. Heinz and a brother began by putting homegrown pickles into jars. They also sold fresh produce from their backyard greenhouse to local grocers. The teenagers' initial investment was 10 cents. When the current family head, a U.S. Senator, was killed in an airplane crash in 1991, the corporation was valued at $10,000,000,000.

Portland, OR, 1963—To make ends meet, an auditor started moonlighting by importing athletic shoes from Japan and selling them out of his station wagon. Talking about the venture with his ex-college coach, the latter made some important improvements to the sneakers and launched the venture. The initial $1,000 investment to import the shoes has now turned into a $3,000,000,000 business. The entrepreneurs are Philip Knight and Bill Bowerman, and their company is Nike, Inc.

Chicago, IL, 1942—Who is the largest African American publisher in the U.S.? John H. Johnson, founder and owner of Johnson Publishing Co. (*Ebony* magazine, et al.). A half a century ago his business was started with $500. How? He took advantage of an existing mailing list of the insurance company for which he worked. He borrowed 20,000 names and mailed a subscription solicitation for a newsletter he planned to publish. As luck would have it, 3,000 replies poured in with checks, and the project was launched. The Johnson publishing empire today is worth nearly $250,000,000.

Louisville, KY, 1907—Two teenagers were making a few dollars each week delivering packages for local merchants. By 1915 they had to think seriously about going into business. Model-Ts had become popular and with a $100 down payment, they bought their first delivery vehicle. Today, a couple of generations later, James Casey's and Claude Ryan's little business has thousands of dark brown trucks all over the country with the name United Parcel Service (UPS) stenciled on each side. The worth of the business? About $6,000,000,000.

New York, NY, 1935—In the midst of the Great Depression, Josephine Esther Mentzer helped out the family by selling a skin-care ointment that her uncle was marketing. Then she got an idea. Rather than selling door-to-door the slow way or to a few local drug stores with little turnover, why not try the high-volume department stores? However, before trying the new outlets, she developed her own line of cosmetics with about $100 in savings. Today these cosmetics are known as Estee Lauder, and the company is worth about $1,000,000,000, making the erstwhile Ms. Mentzer one of the world's richest women.

Recent Companies That Began on a Shoestring
Men's Shorts Produce Long Profits

San Francisco, CA—Joe Boxer Inc., manufacturer of men's boxer shorts and ties, was established by 24-year-old Nicholas Graham with about $100 in capital. Calling on men's clothing stores and men's buyers at local department stores, he sold them unusually patterned ties, which he made himself in his bedroom. One buyer suggested using the unusual fabrics to make boxer shorts, and a new line was born. The first year, Graham wound up with $600,000 gross volume, and financed his growing operation with factoring all orders at 80 percent of invoices on the day an order was shipped. All sewing was eventually subcontracted. Now contracting has been farmed out to a plant in China. After 18 months in business, Joe Boxer Inc. reported volume at the rate of $1,000,000 annually. Eight years later the company had 46 employees and grossed $22,000,000 annually.

Real Estate Billing Starts Newsletter

Houston, TX—As a part-time real estate salesman in college, Marc Ostrofsky was inspired to go into the newsletter business. Using a technique he learned in real estate, he collected the first and last month's payments of the yearly advertising contract, and with this up front money was able to parlay his new business into two magazines. Seven years later, his business was grossing $3,700,000 and employing 30 full- and part-time people.

$30,000,000 Business Forms Firm Started Informally

Cleveland, OH—A trained accountant, Greg Muzzilo, was only twenty-three when he decided that being in business for himself is the only way to go. Everybody, he reasoned, used business forms, though he didn't realize that it's a highly competitive business. The first few hundred dollars of his own money went into telephone answering machines and a decent letterhead. Then he opened a line of credit with 25 different business form manufacturers, and vendors were impressed with his youthful enthusiasm and earnestness. He also developed a tough phone technique, masquerading as an implied mob collector, that he used on recalcitrant customers. Thirteen years later, the company did $30,000,000 annually and employed 65 men and women.

UPS Payments Financed Cheeky Startup

Mequon, WI—When you have great ideas for software packages but are only twenty-one and have but a few hundred dollars in the bank, ingenuity must become a partner. Dan Armbrust used his imagination and cleverness. He bought some floppy discs and put his ingenious programs on the blank diskettes, shrink-wrapped them on a household gadget, and started making cold calls to computer stores. What he sold he collected COD, turning a disk bought for pennies into a retail item sold for as much as $199. He arranged to buy supplies from out-of-state vendors. They then shipped via UPS. Armbrust paid the drivers, but knew he had several days to make good on the checks. Several days' delay was enough to copy the software onto the blank disks, deliver them, and make good on the payments. It was risky, but it worked. Eight years later, the company did $16,000,000 in annual revenue and kept 34 employees on the payroll.

Vietnam Vet Discovers Novelty Business

San Leandro, CA—Living in the back of a warehouse and eking out a meager living by driving a truck and going to school under the G.I. Bill, Fred DaMert tinkered with polymers. His experiments, designed for family Christmas gifts, turned up a real surprise. His soft prisms reflected natural light in wondrous ways and sparked the idea that he had indeed latched on to a salable gift item. A local chain store buyer ordered 24. Others followed. Then he found that museum stores across the country loved his items. For 18 years now, DaMert has been making a good living, as have his 15 employees, and annual business is brisk at about $4,500,000.

Gimmick Business Grows on Brains, Not Bucks

Los Angeles, CA—Marc Sirkin, a twenty-five-year-old production manager for a TV show, figured that tinsel town needed somebody with his fertile brain to come up with promotional gimmicks. So with a few bucks, a spare bedroom, and a few friends, he started making T-shirts, jackets, balloons, and plastic replicas to hype various movies. After two years of struggle, he obtained an order for 15,000 emblazoned jackets at $22 each, a $180,000 order that enabled the mini-company to finance itself into major growth. Ingenuity and quick turnaround of orders sparked the growth, not heavy financing. Today the company provides a living for 15 employees and grosses $3,600,000 a year.

Parlaying Pennies in Disney's Shadow

Orlando, FL—In the shadow of the Walt Disney empire south of Orlando, Florida, a tourists' guide carrying a respectable 64 pages into 200,000 hands is making money for the Kenneys. It wasn't always so, that is, until Dick Kenney, working part-time to support his new idea, started the first of the local tourist newspapers, financed with a month's rent of $185. The copy was done on an old typewriter. A printer accepted the job on spec. The Kenneys did distribution store-to-store. Enough advertisers paid half of their ad costs up front. A decade later, the guides take in $1,000,000 and keep 16 part- and full-time employees busy.

Visors Give Sunny Staff to Student Entrepreneurs

Atlanta, GA—Two college dropouts, restless to get away from theory and into a money-producing business, figured that a good sun visor would sell well in sunny Florida. They pooled their meager funds and drove down to the Sunshine State. Some weeks of market research later, they came up with a plastic visor that clamped around foreheads without straps or elastics. A local mold maker agreed it was a good item and staked the boys to a free mold in return for a two-cent royalty on each of an estimated 1,000,000 visors sold. They called their company Alpha Products and turned a fledgling idea into a $20,000,000 success, generating all sorts of other products along the way to success. How did they finance themselves in the early stages? By moving furniture for local stores.

CHAPTER 3

Assistance and Information

Starters: Where You Should Go First

W here do you start if 1) you currently are not in business and 2) would like to learn how to avoid common pitfalls and 3) want to take advantage of the experience of others?

The following organizations will help point you in the right direction:

The Business Assistance Program, formerly known as The Roadmap Program, guides business to appropriate contacts.

Contact the Business Assistance Office, Department of Commerce, Rm. 5721C, 14th & Constitution Avenue, NW, Washington, DC 20230. Contact (202) 482-3176 or (202) 482-1306; Fax (202) 482-4054.

The Federal Information Center (FIC) can also help you find the right answer. Often they will have copies of commonly-used forms, such as copyright forms, that they will send from a telephoned request. These centers are a focal point for information about the federal government.

Centers assist people who have questions about federal services, programs, and regulations, but do not know where to turn for an answer. FIC information specialists will answer your questions directly, or perform the necessary research to locate and refer the inquirer to the expert best able to help. Call (800) 688-9889, or check out the Web site: http://fic.info.gov

Through workshops, individual counseling, publications, and videotapes, the Small Business Association (SBA) helps entrepreneurs understand and meet the challenges of starting a business, including financing, marketing, and management. The SBA has business development specialists stationed in more than 100 field offices nationwide. Technical assistance, training, and counseling are offered by two partner organizations and numerous walk-in Business Information Centers.

SBA's Business Information Centers (BICs) provide state-of-the-art computers, graphic workstations, CD-ROM technology and interactive videos for accessing market research databases, planning and spreadsheet software, and a vast library of information. With the BIC library and software, you can craft your own business and marketing plans.

SBA's one-stop capital shops gather federal, state and local agencies and institutions in one convenient location to address the financial and technical assistance needs of small businesses.

More than 11,500 volunteers in the Service Corps of Retired Executives (SCORE) provide training and one-on-one counseling at no charge.

Small Business Development Centers provide training, counseling, research and other specialized assistance at nearly 1,000 locations nationwide. (See Appendix 1.)

To find the BIC, SCORE, or Small Business Development Center in your area, check the government section of your phonebook.

The Answer Desk focuses on federal government programs and regulations, but also provides information about state, municipal, and private sector agencies. It does not provide legal, accounting, or managerial advice. They refer such inquiries to appropriate sources, such as lawyers, accountants, SBA field offices, and appropriate government agencies.

The Answer Desk enables the SBA to become aware of the problems and issues of the small business community, which ultimately helps government do a better job of helping small business. Call (800) 827-5722 or, if in the Washington, DC, area, (202) 205-6740.

The Best Problem Solvers

Once you've gathered some basic information or start running into problems, try these fixer-uppers:

Service Corps of Retired Executives (SCORE) assists with free business counseling and training. They can get you out of the red faster than Rambo. SCORE exists solely for the benefit of the small business community. For anyone who is in a small business, or considering entering into one, SCORE offers many services that can be of critical importance to his or her success. SCORE makes no charge for counseling services, but usually charges a nominal fee for participating in training and workshop sessions.

Small business clients should be encouraged to take advantage of any of the following SCORE services that may meet their needs:

- **Counseling:** Both those who are considering entering a business enterprise and those who are already in a small business may benefit from the experience of successful, retired executives who are familiar with similar businesses. The advice furnished by SCORE counselors may be directed toward solving a particular problem or toward planning for future growth.

- **Training:** Broadly focused pre-startup business workshops are offered periodically, as well as more specialized classes, seminars, and conferences concerning topics of great value to certain segments of the business community. Subjects such as business organization, site selection, trade promotion, marketing, accounting, taxation, and financing are a few examples of the specialized training available.

- **Information:** Advice on obtaining and utilizing the professional services of lawyers, accountants, bankers, advertising agencies, and others, as well as the resources of government agencies, is provided upon request.

The primary purpose of SCORE is to render a community service by providing, without charge, the expert assistance of its volunteer counselors in solving the problems encountered by small businesses. In addition to a substantial number of retired executives and managers, the membership of SCORE chapters throughout the country includes many individuals who have not yet retired from active employment. Volunteer counselors who are qualified to furnish specialized counseling and training based upon their extensive and widely-varied business and professional experience are selected.

To locate a SCORE chapter near you, look in the phone book for the nearest SBA office or call (800) 634-0245. You'll receive a recorded list of SCORE phone numbers in your area.

Written inquiries should be addressed to:

SCORE Association
National SCORE Office, 6th Floor
409 3rd Street, SW
Washington, DC 20024-3212.

CHAPTER 4

New Products

License a Government Invention

Each year government laboratories invent hundreds of new items that can be licensed by you, often on an exclusive basis. For example, 27 percent of NASA's patents are turned over to private industry via these agreements. Currently there are over 7,000 patents available for license.

A weekly newsletter, *Government Inventions for Licensing*, presents summaries (abstracts) of new inventions. All inventions are available for licensing (often exclusive). The newsletter describes some 1,200 new inventions each year. Annually, all inventions are presented in the *Catalog of Government Inventions Available for Licensing*. This catalog arranges descriptions of these 1,200 inventions under 41 subject areas for easy reference.

There is also a service named *Tech Notes*. *Tech Notes* provide illustrated monthly fact sheets of new processes and products developed by federal agencies and their contractors. Each fact sheet details a specific invention, process, software, material, instrument or technique selected for its potential for commercial development or practical application. Annual collections of all *Tech Notes* are available as the *Federal Technical Catalog*.

For more information contact: National Technical Information Service (NTIS), Center for the Utilization of Federal Technology

(CUFT), Dept. of Commerce, 5285 Port Royal Rd., Springfield, VA 22161. Telephone (703) 605-6100; Fax (703) 605-6900.

Getting Your Invention Evaluated (And Perhaps Some Cash Too)

If your invention is energy related, you can get a free evaluation of its commercial feasibility and perhaps a grant to develop it further.

The Energy Related Inventions Program encourages innovation in non-nuclear energy technology by helping individual inventors and small R&D companies develop promising energy-related inventions. It evaluates all submitted inventions and recommends those that are promising to the Department of Energy (DOE).

The evaluation criteria are technical feasibility, degree of energy impact, commercial potential, and intrinsic technical merit. DOE then reviews the recommended inventions and, working closely with the inventor, determines the next reasonable step for the invention and how much money it will take. Most often, support takes the form of a one-time-only cash grant and technical assistance in developing linkages with the private sector.

Contact: Industrial Strategies Office, Department of Energy at (202) 586-0139.

Automatic Notification of What's Being Patented Concerning Your Specialty

If you have a particular interest, it's a good idea to keep abreast of what others are doing. Often, after receiving a patent, you may wish to contact the inventors or you might get fresh ideas on improving your product without infringement.

Using the Patent Subscription Service and establishing a deposit account with the Patent and Trademark Office (PTO), businesses can be sent full copies of all appropriate patents as they are issued. Selection is made using any of the more than 112,000 subclasses.

Contact: Patent Publication Office, Department of Commerce, CPK3 2231 Crystal Drive, Arlington, VA 22202. Speak with Richard Baucombe at (703) 305-8594; Fax (703) 305-4372.

How to File for a Patent

The Patent and Trademark Office examines patent applications and grants protection for qualified inventions. It also collects, assembles, and disseminates the technological information disclosed on patent grants.

Printed copies of individual patents may be purchased directly from PTO. Printed collections of all new patents are issued each week in the *Official Gazette,* which is available, by subscription from the Government Printing Office.

A booklet, *General Information Concerning Patents,* is available from the Superintendent of Documents, Washington, DC 20402 for $2 or by calling (202) 512-0571. An information booklet, *Basic Facts about Patents,* is available from the Patent Office.

Contact: Public Affairs Office, Patent and Trademark Office, Dept. of Commerce, 2011 Crystal Drive, Arlington, VA 22202. For customer service call (703) 305-7604.

Registering A Trademark

Businesses interested in registering a trademark may contact the trademark information office for the information and forms required. An information booklet, *Basic Facts About Trademarks,* is available.

Applications for trademark registration must be filed in the name of the owner of the mark. The owner may file his own application for registration, or he may be represented by an attorney. Trademark applications may be filed before a trademark has been used. However, protection is reduced from 20 to 10 years. It may be re-registered after that period.

Contact: Trademark Information, Patent and Trademark Office, Department of Commerce, 2900 Crystal Drive, Arlington, VA 22202-3513. Telephone (703) 308-9500; Fax (703) 308-9395.

Obtaining a Copyright

A series of pamphlets and forms is available to assist firms in understanding, searching, or applying for a copyright. Although the office cannot give legal advice, it can assist in providing information on claiming a copyright, what can be copyrighted, notice of copyright, transfer of a copyright, and searching records of the Copyright Office.

Contact: Copyright Office, Library of Congress, Washington, DC 20559. Telephone (202) 707-3000.

Where To Get Information on Foreign Research

Technology-oriented businesses interested in staying up to date with foreign government technology will find the efforts of the Foreign Technology Program of special value. NTIS maintains formal agreements with more than 90 foreign sources of technical reports. In addition, NTIS receives foreign technical reports collected by other U.S. Government agencies. In all, some 20,000 foreign reports are annually added to the NTIS report collection.

A bi-weekly newsletter provides useful information gathered from embassy and other sources around the world. Included in the newsletter are abstracts to the current foreign R&D results.

The countries covered by this program include Austria, Australia, Belgium, Canada, Denmark, Finland, France, Germany, Israel,

Japan, the Netherlands, New Zealand, Norway, South Africa, Sweden, Switzerland, and the United Kingdom. Most of the reports from these countries are available in English.

Contact: Foreign Technology Program, National Technical Information Service (NTIS), Department of Commerce, 5285 Port Royal Road, Room 305, Springfield, VA 22161. Telephone (703) 605-6534; Fax (703) 605-6742.

How to Develop and Bring a New Product to Market

The Departments of Energy and Commerce, the National Society of Professional Engineers, the National Congress of Inventor Organizations, the Licensing Executives Society, and the American Intellectual Property Law Association sponsor two-day seminars throughout the U.S. The topics covered are: patenting and protection, estimating the worth of an invention, licensing, marketing, new business startup, your business plan, research and development, venture financing, and the Department of Energy's Inventions Program and Small Business Innovative Research Programs.

If your new product is energy related, the Department of Energy may provide assistance in developing, financing, and marketing the product. The seminar applies to all products, whether or not they're energy related.

If you desire more information, contact: Office of Technology Innovation, National Institute of Standards and Technology (formerly National Bureau of Standards), Building 820, Room 306, Gaithersburg, MD 20899-0001. Telephone (301) 975-4510.

Help to Stimulate the Innovative Process

The Small Business Technology Liaison Division and the Industrial Technology Partnership Division work with smaller firms to assist them to better understand the components of the innovative process. They focus on a company's understanding of business tools such as sensitivity analysis, technology screening, and networking resources. They can connect you with other groups involved in innovation.

Training is also provided in R&D (innovation) financing mechanisms and in the innovation process. Training, for individuals and small groups, is customized to the requester's needs. It covers: innovation policy; cooperative and joint R&D arrangements; R&D limited partnerships; corporate partnering; federal and national R&D funding; sources of cooperation between universities and industry; venture capital; and innovation facilitators. A series of special publications is available.

Contact: Office of Technology Commercialization, Department of Commerce, Bldg 820, Route 207, Gaithersburg, MD 20899. Telephone (301) 975-3084; Fax (301) 869-2751.

Stuff Made Out of Wood

It may surprise you to find that the U.S. Forest Service serves the private sector with its research to improve the use of wood and to develop wood products.

Its Forest Product Laboratory in Madison, Wisconsin, has developed wood structures such as the truss-framed system, an innovative way to build homes and light commercial buildings. The system uses 30 percent less structural framing than conventional construction, can be put up faster by fewer people, and is more disaster resistant.

Builders could realize a savings in construction costs. It has been used in 31 states so far and its use is spreading. The system has been assigned a public patent and can be used by anyone.

A recent product concept is a lightweight structural fiber panel called FPL Spaceboard, which is molded from wood fibers. It can be made thinner, lighter, and stronger than existing fiber boards. It may have uses in wall, floor, and roof panels, in packaging, and in some furniture applications. The spaceboard concept offers you a way to use virgin or recycled wood fiber.

The Forest Products Laboratory has publications to meet the needs of many users. There are publications' lists of interest to furniture manufacturers. architects, engineers, builders, and lumber retailers. Other lists cover: packaging (boxes, crates, pallets), adhesives, wood energy (including research on liquid fuels), finishing wood exteriors, fire performance of wood, and wood drying. Materials are also available on subjects such as improvement of sawmill efficiency and recycling of paper and wood wastes.

For more information, write or call Public Affairs Specialist, Forest Products Laboratory, One Gifford Pinchot Drive, Madison, WI, 53705-2398. Telephone (608) 231-9240 or (608) 231-9200; Fax (608) 231-9592.

Building a Manufacturing Advantage

The Manufacturing Engineering Laboratory (MEL) at the National Institute of Standards and Technology serves as a central research laboratory for manufacturing infrastructure technology, measurements, and standards. They provide industry-needed manufacturing engineering tools, interface standards, manufacturing systems architectures, and traceability. For example, the industrial measurements of length, force, mass, acoustics, vibration, and product data exchange ultimately rely on traceability to MEL.

Through their research and services, MEL sustains a solid record of helping U.S. industry successfully compete in the global marketplace. Manufacturers employ MEL research results, test methods, software conformance tests, calibration services, and measurement tools. They collaborate on technical projects, standards development, and testbed-based research, both on an individual basis and as members of industrial consortia. They also play a key role in fostering intercompany cooperation and industrial adoption of strategically important manufacturing and computing hardware, equipment, and software standards.

Research particularly benefits the discrete-parts manufacturing sector. MEL's work on characterizing and controlling machining processes enables this sector to improve dramatically its tools, processes, and products. Efforts in the area of intelligent machines and systems are accelerating the trend toward open systems architecture and intelligent manufacturing.

Over a decade ago, MEL launched the Automated Manufacturing Research Facility, a pioneering testbed for collaborative research. The goal was to develop and apply the measurements and standards needed to integrate the individual machines, workstations, and functions of a factory into a smoothly operating whole. This testbed provided a path to the present state of computer-integrated manufacturing.

The present challenge is to achieve more demanding levels of precision; another is to optimize systems and control processes more closely, to achieve better product reliability and quality. Without better reliability and quality at reasonable cost, U.S. manufacturers will be left behind in the global economic race.

To help manufacturers keep a lead in this race, MEL inaugurated a state-of-the-art National Advanced Manufacturing Testbed (NAMT). Using the NAMT, research partners and NIST remotely access and share information, demonstrate manufacturing feasibility, and evaluate prototype standards. The NAMT provides the means to conduct distributed and virtual manufacturing research in advanced metrology, control, and interoperability technology. The results will create a new information technology-based manufacturing model.

This is an era where customer demands force manufacturers to satisfy changing technical requirements. MEL is helping with new manufacturing and information technologies, improved measurement capabilities, and advanced standards. They provide the underlying technical infrastructure necessary to meet today's needs and tomorrow's challenges.

Contact: Manufacturing Engineering Laboratory, Bldg 220, Route 270, Gaithersburg, MD 20899. Telephone (301) 975-3401; Fax (301) 948-5668.

The Manufacturing Extension Partnership (MEP)

The Manufacturing Extension Partnership (MEP)—a program of the Department of Commerce's National Institute of Standards and Technology—is a growing network of services to assist smaller manufacturers in becoming globally competitive. MEP partners federal support with state and local organizations. Services are locally-driven so that they address the specific needs of area manufacturers. At the same time, MEP is developing common tools and resources to address recurring and consistent challenges faced by all manufacturers nationwide.

MEP helps small manufacturers overcome barriers to change, so that they may adopt contemporary technologies and business practices, is the role of the Manufacturing Extension Partnership. The following documents are available to help you make use of MEP:

Frequently Asked Questions: Questions and answers about MEP, such as "Do Other Countries Have Similar Programs?," "What are typical projects?" and "How do you measure the results?"

In Perspective: An outline describing MEP and putting it in economic, political and historical perspective.

Making a Difference for America's Manufacturers: This describes MEP in more detail and provides information about the services and programs MEP provides.

The General Accounting Office (GAO) obtained U.S. manufacturers' opinions regarding the services they received from manufacturing extension programs. For further information:

Manufacturing Extension Partnership, 100 Bureau Drive, MS1000, National Institute of Standards and Technology, Gaithersburg, MD 20899-0001. Telephone (301) 975-5454; Fax (301) 990-6492. E-mail: MEPinfo@micf.nist.gov

Web site: http://www.mep.nist.gov/

Factory of the Future

The Center for Manufacturing Engineering operates the National Advanced Manufacturing Testbed. The main purpose is to address two basic problems in computer-integrated manufacturing:

> Provide assurance that small firms will be able to obtain equipment from different manufacturers at different times and have them all work together without expensive custom-designed interfaces.

> Find means of controlling quality in a fully automated factory by innovative measurement processes.

Dozens of companies, large and small, have sent their researchers to work in this facility beside their government counterparts. The results have been voluntary standards that are solving the compatibility problem.

In addition, over 36 patents, products, and systems have found their way into commercial use as a result of work at the NAMT.

All machines and computer systems used in the NAMT are made in the U.S. It is expected that 100,000 machine shops, mostly small ones, will take advantage of this automation technology.

At one time, the U.S. suffered on quality of manufacture products. NAMT techniques are revolutionizing the manufacturing process to make sure parts are made right the first time and every time. All this is accomplished faster, with less waste, with a set-up time of nearly zero.

Tours through this exemplary facility in Gaithersburg, Maryland, may be arranged. Contact: Manufacturing Engineering Laboratory, Bldg 220, Route 270, Gaithersburg, MD 20899. Telephone (301) 975-6100; Fax (301) 948-5668 or (301) 926-8730.

Shop of the Future

Small machine shops fabricate 75 percent of all U.S. metal products. However, they are behind countries such as Japan, Sweden, and Germany in use of modern technology.

Uncle Sam has set up a program to help solve automation problems. Questions such as:

- What modern technologies are commercially available, affordable, and useful to small job shops?
- What return on investment might be expected?
- Where can shop personnel get training?

The Fabrication Technology Division of the National Institute of Standards and Technology (NIST) has created a shop similar to a small, privately-owned operation. Only affordable off-the-shelf systems and software are used. Purchases and changes are justified by a reasonable return on investment.

The program reviews and evaluates existing machine tools and resources, uses personal computers for cost estimates, planning, computer aided design and manufacturing, and trains shop personnel in the use of this system.

One example is the U.S. Olympic Ski Team, which uses aerodynamic helmets manufactured by small shops from a diskette provided by NIST. The helmet has less drag, is twice as light and four times as strong as the team's previous helmet.

A seminar center with hardware and software has been established. The center is available to private industry.

For more information contact: Fabrication Technology Division, Manufacturing Engineering Laboratory, National Institute of Standards and Technology, Building 304, Room 136, Gaithersburg, MD 20898. Telephone (301) 975-6504; Fax (301) 921-2079.

To get the new number, call the toll-free Federal Information Number (800) 688-9889. The operator will give you the new number for the agency you need.

CHAPTER 5

Selling to the Feds

(Or, How to Get Your Tax Money Back)

U ncle Sam can be your best customer; there is no product or service that he doesn't purchase someplace. One of the following should help you contract with Uncle Sam:

The Commerce Business Daily (CBD) lists notices of proposed government procurement actions, contract awards, sales of government property, and other procurement information. Notices of contract actions that appear in the CBD are arranged by classification codes. The classification codes are divided into two primary groups, Services and Supplies. You may:

- Search the *Commerce Business Daily* using the service codes
- Search the *Commerce Business Daily* using the supply codes
- Create your own free-form search

Contact your library or the Department of Commerce office. To subscribe for the service ($324 annual fee) call (202) 512-1530.

Defense Logistics Agency (DLA)—Procurement leads are a consolidation of small purchase opportunities (less than $25,000) from six DLA procurement centers. Telephone (703) 767-1400; Fax (703) 767-1588.

If your product consists of supplies, sofas, software, phones or floorsweepers: In case you have a common-use service or item for sale, ask the U.S. General Services Administration's (GSAs) Small Business Specialists at the nearest GSA Business Service Center for help. These centers are located in GSA regional offices around the United States:

GSA Business Services Centers

California
300 N. Los Angeles Street, Room 3259
Los Angeles, CA 90012
(213) 894-3210

450 Golden Gate Ave., Room 6514
San Francisco, CA 94102
(415) 522-2700

Colorado
Room 141, Bldg 41
Denver Federal Center
P.O. Box 25006
Denver, CO 80225-0006
(303) 236-7408

District of Columbia
Seventh & D Streets SW
Washington, DC 20407
202) 708-5804

Georgia
401 W. Peachtree Street, Room 2800
Atlanta, GA 30303-2550
(404) 331-5103

Illinois

230 S. Dearborn Street
Chicago, IL 60604
(312) 353-5383

Massachusetts

O'Neill Federal Office Bldg.
10 Causeway Street
Boston MA 02222-1093
(617) 565-8100

Missouri

1500 E. Bannister Road
Kansas City, MO 64131
(816) 926-7203

New York

Javits Federal Bldg.
26 Federal Plaza
New York, NY 10278
(212) 264-1234

Pennsylvania

Wanamaker Bldg.
100 Penn Square, Room 808
East Philadelphia, PA 19107
(215) 656-5525

Texas

819 Taylor Street, Room 11A09
Fort Worth TX 76102
817) 978-3284

Washington

Room 2413, GSA Center
400 15th Street SW
Auburn, WA 98001
(206) 931-7956

The Business Service Center staff works with suppliers of goods and services to provide more than 4 million products and services for federal agencies. The kinds of items provided include: office supplies and equipment, computers and software, furniture, tools, hardware, refrigerators, air-conditioners, water coolers, scientific and laboratory equipment, medical, photographic equipment, and audio-video recording equipment and supplies.

Procurements are made under several programs within the Federal Supply Service, Public Buildings Service and Federal Telecommunications Service.

Federal Supply Service

Stock Program: Under this program, over 13,000 common-use items are procured in bulk, stored and redistributed to federal customers through a worldwide distribution system of four full-service distribution centers and seven stand-alone customer supply centers.

Federal Supply Schedule Programs are centralized contracts established for the use of all federal agencies. They cover either goods or services ordered directly by federal customers and delivered directly to them by private-sector vendors. They provide federal agencies with sources for products and services such as computer hardware and software, telecommunications products, furniture, electric lamps, appliances, photographic, duplicating, athletic, laboratory, and audio and video recording equipment and supplies. Schedules are indefinite-quantity contracts entered into with commercial firms to provide supplies and services at stated prices for given periods of time. They permit agencies to place orders directly with suppliers. Federal Supply Schedules are published to provide ordering data for these contracts.

Special Order Program: Items sometimes are not suitable for inclusion in either the Stock or Federal Supply Schedule programs. These include vehicles and other products for which demand is limited or related to special needs, or those for which stocking is not desirable but consolidated ordering is beneficial. GSA consolidates agency requirements for such items and special definite quantity contracts are executed. Direct delivery is made from the contractor to the agency involved. Information is available on supplying items for these programs and placement on a bidders mail list.

The products and services provided through these programs can be procured by automated ordering, telephone, mail or via the Internet. FSS recently initiated its GSA Advantage!™ 24-hour on-line ordering system, where you can shop for items (www.gsa.gov), select delivery options, place your order electronically, and pay with a government charge card or account number.

Public Buildings Service (PBS)

Leasing Services: PBS leases general-purpose space for federal agencies throughout the country. It also leases special-purpose space, such as laboratories and clinics, for any agency that requests it. Leases cover space ranging in size from a single room to an entire building.

Construction Services: PBS contracts with small businesses for many services needed in construction and maintenance of public buildings. These include construction, electrical, plumbing, heating, and air conditioning and special trade contractors.

Design Excellence Program: PBS contracts for architect/engineer services for federal office buildings, courthouses, and research centers; mechanical and electrical systems and elevators; engineering specialties; repairs and alterations to existing buildings and renovation of historical structures.

Building Cleaning and Maintenance: These include building cleaning (interior), building maintenance, floor waxing, window cleaning, venetian blind cleaning, lighting maintenance (bulb replacement and cleaning), and janitorial services.

Security Services: PBS contracts with a number of small businesses to provide building security guards. Thousands of contract guards provide security at federal facilities.

Federal Telecommunications Services: FTS contracts with providers of local and long-distance telecommunications services under several programs:

- Aggregated System Procurements (ASPs) and Individual System Procurements (ISPs) for voice and data telecommunications;

- Metropolitan Area Acquisitions (MAAs) of local telecommunications services;

- Purchase of Telecommunications Services (POTS) for telecommunications equipment, installation, design assistance and user training;

- International Direct Distance Dialing (ID3)

- Commerce, Internet, Electronic-Mail Access (CINEMA)

In addition, FTS contracts for technical and management support, planning, requirements analysis, design and engineering, integration, and installation and implementation support.

Information Technology Integration: The FTS Information Technology Integration programs are centers of expertise that provide a wide range of services related to information systems and information technology, and a wide range of opportunities for contractors.

Federal Information Systems Support Program (FISSP) contracts for systems definition and design, business and scientific software services, computer security studies and risk analyses, facilities management and other related services.

Federal Systems Integration and Management Center (FEDSIM) contracts for data processing services; information systems, and information technology; comprehensive services for addressing year 2000 date-change issues; data center disaster recovery services and automated information systems security services.

Federal Acquisition Support for Technology (FAST) buys commercially available off-the-shelf information technology software, equipment, services, and non-complex integration services.

Federal Computer Acquisition Center (FEDCAC) delivers full-service management of computer acquisitions worth more than $100 million.

Call your nearest Business Service Center or (202) 708-5804.

Selling by the Internet

The Procurement Automated Source System (PASS) has been replaced by the Electronic Commerce Resource Center (ECRC). Beginning in January 1999, all procurements under $100,000 are required to use ECRC.

Get easy exposure for your products and capabilities to all federal agencies. ECRC substantially improves government contract and subcontract opportunities for small business. There are 16 regional ECRC's to help you. To find the one for your area call (800) 691-3867 or fax (703) 691-8948 or contact your closest SBA office.

Procurement Information

You can contact the Federal Procurement Data Center in Washington to obtain procurement information customized for your needs. The center is a unique source of consolidated information about federal purchases; its information can assist businesses in their planning and marketing efforts. A master database contains detailed information on the purchases by more than sixty agencies. You can learn how much the government spent in each fiscal quarter on items such as clothing, food, furniture, fuel, building materials, ADP services, and weapons. Two types of reports are available to you:

A no-cost standard report contains statistical procurement information in snapshot form. It also compares procurement activities by state, major product and service codes, degree of competition, and contractors.

Special reports tailored to your specific need are also available. They can be based upon up to 25 data elements that can be cross-tabulated in hundreds of ways. Such a report can help you to analyze government procurement data and trends, identify competitors, and locate federal markets for your products or services.

Information provided to you in a special report can include the names of federal agency purchasing offices, products or services, and the dates agreements were reached, contractors' names and addresses, dollar amounts obligated, extent of competition, and types of businesses that received an award. Examples include:

- who purchased and sold traffic signal systems
- awards to a specific corporation
- construction contracting by state
- contract awards for specific counties or states
  the top 300 contractors of the Department of Defense
  (DOD) for R&D contracts the top 200 product codes
  ranked by dollars awarded

On a reimbursable basis the center will also provide you with computer tapes of the entire contents of its database; mailing lists of contractors who sell to the government sorted by region, product, and service code, et al., and mailing lists of federal purchasing offices.

You may call or write: General Services Administration, Federal Computer Acquisition Center, 5203 Leesburg Pike, Falls Church, VA 22041. Telephone (202) 501-1568; Fax (703) 756-6167.

Department of Defense Potential Contractors

If you want to try defense projects, join the Potential Contractor Program. The program certifies and registers non-government organizations for access to Department of Defense (DOD) scientific and technical information. This includes information on needs, requirements, work, and accomplishments associated with research, development, test, and evaluation. Through this program, organizations are provided the opportunity and means to obtain current scientific and technical information required to maintain their capabilities as developers and producers of military equipment and matériel.

Firms, individuals or activities with a demonstrable capability of performing research/development with a reasonable potential for eventually receiving a contract with DOD are invited to participate in the program.

For all services, contact: Director Defense Research & Engineering, 3030 Defense Pentagon Washington, DC 20301-3030. Telephone (703) 695-0598; Fax (703) 614-0823.

You may become certified as "competent" through the Certificate of Competency Program. This program will certify a small company's capability, competency, credit, integrity, perseverance, and tenacity to perform a specific government contract. If a federal contracting officer proposes to reject the bid of a small business firm that is a low bidder because he questions the firm's ability to perform the contract on any of the above grounds, the case is referred to the SBA. SBA personnel then contact you to inform you of the impending decision, and to offer you an opportunity to apply to SBA for a Certificate of Competency (COC), which, if granted, would require award of the contract to your firm in accordance with the Small Business Act.

SBA may also, at its discretion, issue a COC in connection with the sale of federal property if the responsibility (capacity, credit, integrity, tenacity, and perseverance) of the purchaser is questioned, and for firms found ineligible by a contracting officer due to a provision of the Walsh-Healey Public Contracts Act which requires that a government contractor be either a manufacturer or a regular dealer.

Contact: Office of Industrial Assistance, Small Business Administration, 8th Floor, 409 3rd Street SW, Washington, DC 20416. Telephone (202) 205-6475; Fax (202) 205-7324.

Department of Agriculture

Procurement procedures are explained in the booklet *Selling to USDA*. This publication contains information on who does the buying, the types of items bought for the various programs, and where the buying is done. Included is a directory of purchasing offices and their locations. You may obtain a copy from: Department of Agriculture, Procurement Division, Room 1550, South Bldg., Washington, DC 20215. Telephone (202) 720-7527.

Department of Commerce

Procurement procedures are explained in the booklet *How to Sell to the Department of Commerce*. This publication contains information on who-buys-what-where. Included is a directory of purchasing offices and their locations. You may obtain a copy from: General Procurement Division, Department of Commerce,

14th & Constitution Avenue NW, Room H6516, Washington DC 20230. Telephone (202) 482-5555.

Department of Energy

The Procurement Operations Office handles acquisitions, grants, cooperative agreements, loan guarantees and other financial assistance instruments, management and operating contracts, personal property management, sales contracts, small business/small disadvantaged business/labor surplus area acquisitions, and other business activities.

The procurement procedures of the department are explained in *Doing Business with the Department of Energy*. This publication contains information on who does the buying, the types of items, and where the buying is done. Included is a directory of purchasing offices and their locations. You may obtain a copy from: Department of Energy, Procurement and Assistance Management Directorate, Code: MA 451, 1000 Independence Avenue SW, Washington DC 20585. Telephone (202) 586-1368; Fax (202) 586-3165.

Department of Housing and Urban Development

The booklet *Doing Business with HUD* explains HUD's mission, major programs, and the procurement opportunities it creates, both directly through HUD and indirectly through state and local governments and other organizations which receive financial assistance from the department.

Also included is a brief description of HUD's procurement procedures, a directory of purchasing offices, and an explanation of HUD's Procurement Opportunity Programs for minority, women-owned businesses.

You may obtain a copy from: Procurement and Contracts Office, Department of Housing and Urban Development, Room 5260, 451 Seventh Street SW, Washington, DC 20410. Telephone (202) 708-1290.

Environmental Protection Agency

The procurement procedures are explained in *Doing Business with EPA*. This booklet will aid a business in its efforts to acquire contract work with EPA. It contains information on contact points, addresses and telephone numbers of contracting offices, and describes the types of products and services generally acquired by the EPA.

Contact: Environmental Protection Agency, Washington, DC 20460. Telephone (202) 564-4310.

Department of the Treasury

The procurement procedures are explained in *Selling to the Department of the Treasury*. This publication contains information on who does the buying, the types of items bought for the various programs, and where the buying is done. Included is a directory of purchasing offices and their locations.

Copies are available from Department of Treasury, Room 6100 Treasury Annex, Washington, DC 20220. Telephone (202) 622-1300.

Veterans Administration

You should request the booklet *Could You Use a Multibillion Dollar Customer?*, which contains everything you need to know about this lucrative market.

Contact: Procurement and Supply Services Office, Department of Veteran Affairs, 810 Vermont Avenue N.W., Washington DC 20420. Telephone (202) 273-8792 or (202) 273-5422.

CHAPTER 6

Everything You Ever Wanted to Know, but Were Ashamed to Ask

Customized Economic Research

Customized data is available to you from an economic model designed to measure the impacts of private sector developments and of government programs. Some of the variables included are output, employment, wage rates, population, government revenues, retail sales, investment, and labor force. The model can be used to analyze regional distribution of policy or economic impacts. It assures that the sum of regional activities is consistent with forecasts of national activity.

You can also obtain special data showing the economic effects of potential projects on specific regions. The system offers estimates of economic impact multipliers for 500 industries for any county or group of counties in the United States.

Some examples of the use of the Regional Input-Output Modeling System include: determination of the effect that new warehouse construction would have on personal earnings, assessing the employment effects of various types of urban redevelopment expenditures, the economic impact of port facility expansion, or the effects of new plants on regional private-sector economic activity.

Contact: Bureau of Economic Analysis, Dept. of Commerce, Room 6006, 1441 L Street, NW, Washington, DC 20230. Dial (202) 606-9221 or (202) 606-9246; Fax (202) 606-5311.

Economics and Statistics Administration

Much of the statistical, economic, and demographic information collected by the federal government is made available to the public through the bureaus and offices of the Department of Commerce that are known collectively as the Economics and Statistics Administration (ESA).

Departments or Workgroups:

The Bureau of the Census—known as the nation's factfinder—conducts most surveys for other departments as well as the Department of Commerce. Most of the data in its periodic economic indicators is derived from surveys of businesses and most of the demographic information comes from surveys of households or the decennial census.

The Bureau of Economic Analysis—BEA is the nation's accountant, integrating and interpreting a tremendous volume of data to draw a complete and consistent picture of the U.S. economy. BEA's economic accounts—national, regional, and international—provide information on such key issues as economic growth, regional development, and the nation's position in the world economy.

STAT-USA is a giant information service providing economic, business, and social/environmental program data produced by more than 50 federal sources. It already delivers hundreds of thousands of federal publications and statistical reports to U.S. businesses and the public.

The Bureau of Economic Analysis (BEA)—Much of BEA's work involves taking the basic economic reports, as well as information from many other sources, and constructing the domestic, international, and regional economic accounts.

Contact Information: E-mail: stat-usa@doc.gov
Web site: www.doc.gov/agencies/esa/index.html
Tel: (202) 606-9602

Just for Fun

Just for Fun is designed to give you a "hands on" opportunity in using data and geographic information available from the U.S. Bureau of the Census. You can use Just for Fun to learn a little about statistical information and the tools used to process them or you can just have some fun at this location on the Census Bureau's site. Just for Fun presently features the Census Bureau's Map Stats, an interactive site that presents statistical profiles for states, congressional districts, and counties as well as detailed maps for counties.

Clicking on a series of pages, you can select the U.S. state of your interest, region of the state, and then county. From the county page, you can select: an "expandable" map of the county, STF1A and STF3A tables—1990 census data for the county, USA counties—Data from a variety of sources for the county. County Business Patterns—Data from the 1994 County Business Patterns, an annual publication series. Go to the Census Bureau Web site at www.census.gov

Correct in Every Weigh

The Office of Weights and Measures (OWM) provides leadership and technical resources to obtain uniformity among the states in weights and measures standards, laws, and practices and to facilitate trade and protect U.S. businesses and citizens in sales of products or services totaling over $3.3 trillion annually. OWM sponsors the National Conference on Weights and Measures (NCWM), an organization of state weights and measures officials and representatives of industry, consumers, and federal agencies. The NCWM develops uniform laws, regulations, and methods of practice that are published by NIST. These standards become mandatory when adopted by government regulatory agencies.

OWM manages the State Laboratory Program, which provides the basis for ensuring traceability of state weights and measures standards to NIST. OWM also oversees the National Type Evaluation Program, which evaluates models of commercial weighing and measuring equipment to determine compliance with NIST Handbook 44. It provides training to U.S. and foreign meteorologists and weights and measures officials, and administers the NCWM National Training Program.

Contact: Office of Weights and Measures, National Institute of Standards and Technology, U.S. Department of Commerce, NIST North (Bldg 820), Room 223, Gaithersburg, MD 20899. Telephone (301) 975-4005; Fax (301) 948-3825. Fax-on-demand information system 1-800-925-2453 (information on weights and measures publications and activities available 24 hours a day). Web page: www.nist.gov/owm

Business Statistics 24 Hours a Day, 365¼ Days a Year

Four special telephone lines allow businesses to call any hour of the day to get recorded information on major economic statistics. The index of leading indicators recording includes the levels and percentage changes for the latest three months for the leading indicators. Also included is the contribution that changes in each of the dozen statistical series made to the overall index.

Another recording carries information on two other quarterly statistics, merchandise trade on a balance of payments basis, and U.S. international transactions.

A third number handles the Gross National Product figures. Details of personal income and outlays are available on the fourth telephone line.

Call (202) 606-9722, Bureau of Income and Wealth, for leading indicator statistics, gross national product statistics, personal income, and outlay statistics, and for merchandise trade or U.S. international transactions.

Using Census Data for Your Business

Owners and operators of small businesses often find statistics from the Census Bureau to be of value in such activities as selecting the best location for a new store, deciding on target areas for advertising, determining an appropriate share of the market, and assessing business competition. Census statistics contribute to planning and decision making in these activities through helping business people determine how many potential customers there are in an area, what the dollar value of sales is in merchandise lines of interest to them, what volume of business is done by specific types of businesses, and the answers to related questions.

Included in Census Bureau reports are statistics showing the number of people in defined areas by age, race, sex, occupation, income, and other characteristics; the number of households and selected housing information, including housing value and rent; business activity and industrial production; imports/exports, and other information that may be useful to you.

Data from the censuses are generally presented for cities, metropolitan areas, counties, states, regions, and the nation. In addition, the Census of Population and Housing is the source of data for much smaller areas, such as city blocks and census tracts (small areas roughly equivalent to neighborhoods).

Contact: Bureau of the Census, Department of Commerce, Customer Service Branch, Washington, DC 20233. Telephone (301) 457-1305. You may also contact Regional Census offices.

Federal Help on Automating Your Business

A critical element of the U.S. industrial base, both civilian and military, is the 130,000 small manufacturing firms that have traditionally supplied 70 percent of the component parts to our largest manufacturers. They are under intense competitive pressure from overseas suppliers.

The elements of that competition they must contend with are:

- world-class quality

- price

- just-in-time delivery

- rapid response to changing market needs and new technologies.

The challenges that small manufacturing businesses face:

- most do not truly understand that they are competing in global markets.

- they do not know about off-the-shelf Flexible Computer Integrated Manufacturing (FCIM) systems, which offer one key potential solution. FCIM provides small batch production of a wide variety of products, with almost no downtime, with the same per-unit cost for batches of 1 or 1,000.

- many small firm owners are not computer literate and so are afraid of FCIM.

- the cost can be prohibitive for an individual firm attempting to adopt FCIM.

- most CEOs do not know how to manage a firm using FCIM as a tool.

To help small firms cope with these problems, the Department of Commerce's Office of Productivity, Technology, and Innovation developed a business financing/management/transition technique called shared FCIM. This consists of a manufacturing service center that has state-of-the-art/off-the-shelf Flexible Manufacturing Systems (FMS) systems that lease manufacturing time to small firms.

This is the same technique used by mainframe computer manufacturers to introduce computers to the business community in the 1950s. However, it became clear that retraining of management and work, whether it was leased or used in-house, that the business aspects of FCIM must be understood.

The result was the development of the Teaching Factory, which combines the manufacturing service center and a comprehensive educational component for management and work force.

The resulting benefits include: immediate competitive manufacturing capability with no large up-front costs, strategic planning for the appropriate degree of automation, training of management and work force before making an investment, testing of systems to assure they meet individual firm needs and fast utilization of capacity when firms install their own equipment.

A short mention of the program in the Kiplinger Washington Letter resulted in 450 requests for information. Based on current estimates some 200 shared FCIMs are envisioned in the next decade.

Key points for you to remember are:

- Flexible manufacturing automation may well be critical to the survival of your small manufacturing businesses.

- Only a small percentage of small firms have begun to automate—most without a long-term strategy.

Your understanding of the true business impact of automation is key to its adoption and effective use.

Contact: Office of Technology Commercialization, U.S. Department of Commerce, Room 4418, Washington, D.C. 20230. Telephone (202) 482-1091; Fax (202) 501-2492.

Manufacturing Centers

The Manufacturing Technology Centers Program helps small- and medium-size companies implement automated manufacturing technology. The National Institute of Standards and Technology provides planning and operating funds to the centers, along with participation in cooperative exchanges of modern technology. Advanced manufacturing techniques and methods for fostering their use that are successful at one center are generally available for use in the centers and businesses throughout the nation.

Contact: Manufacturing Technology Centers Program, National Institute of Standards and Technology (formerly National Bureau of Standards), Department of Commerce, Building 224, Room Bl15, Gaithersburg, MD 20899. Telephone (301) 975-6100; Fax (301) 948-5668.

Flexible Manufacturing Systems Program

This program provides basic data on concepts related to financing methods and organizational structures that can make automation a realistic option for small- and medium-sized manufacturers. Information is provided on computer-integrated manufacturing, and especially on automated, flexible manufacturing systems. They will consult with you on your problem.

Contact: Flexible Manufacturing Systems Program, Office of Productivity, Technology and Innovation, Department of

Commerce, Bldg. 233, Gaithersburg, MD 20899. Telephone (301) 975-6600; Fax (301) 948-5668.

Easy Access to Price and Cost Data

Information is available to you that helps evaluate consumer, producer, export, and import prices and price changes. The Bureau of Labor Statistics provides the actual data and assistance in using this data for two major economic indexes: the consumer price index (CPI) and the producer price index (PPI). This office prepares a series of regularly issued publications. The major titles are *Consumer Price Index, Producer Price Index, Export Price Index,* and *Import Price Index.* Recorded messages offer:

- general CPI and employment data (202) 606-7000 and (202) 606-5702
- detailed CPI data (202) 606-6950; detailed producer price data (202) 606-6898.

Contact: Bureau of Labor Statistics, Department of Labor, 2 Massachusetts Avenue NE, Washington DC 20212-4225. Telephone (202) 606-5886 or (202) 606-7800; Fax (202) 606-7797. Web site: http://stats.bls.gov

Productivity Indexes for Your Industry

Indexes of productivity for more than 150 industries are published each year. The factors underlying productivity movements also are carried out. Comparison of U.S. and foreign productivity are available. Comparative productivity measures for the total economy and the iron and steel industry and other labor economic indicators—hourly compensation costs, unit labor costs, prices, employment and unemployment, industrial dispute activity, and other selected measures are prepared.

Employment and occupational implications of technological change and technological changes emerging among selected U.S. industries and the technological innovations such as computers are available. In addition, in-depth studies including data on dissemination of technology are prepared periodically for selected major industries where significant changes are taking place on a large scale.

Contact: Bureau of Labor Statistics, Department of Labor, 2 Massachusetts Avenue NE, Washington DC 20212-4225. Telephone (202) 606-5618 or (202) 606-7800; Fax (202) 606-7797. Web site: http://stats.bls.gov

Finding Out How You Can Compare with the Competition

The Interfirm Productivity Comparisons (IPC) program is a method for a group of managers of competing firms in the same industry to receive confidential productivity report cards based on a set of approximately 30 critical operating and financial ratios. Participants also receive numerical class ranks describing how their firm compares with competitors.

In addition, organizations sponsoring interfirm comparisons projects (e.g. trade associations) are given summary analyses useful for policy or program initiatives in behalf of the industry.

The Office of Technology Commercialization offers you technical assistance, explanations of the concept, and basic information you need before undertaking an Interfirm Productivity Comparison. This OPTI service is provided to groups of companies principally through such intermediary vehicles as trade associations.

Contact: Interfirm Productivity Comparisons Program, Office of Technology Commercialization, Bldg 820, Route 270, Gaithersburg, MD 20899. Telephone (301) 975-4510; Fax (301) 869-2183.

Information on Radio, TV and Telecommunications

The Office of Policy Analysis and Development will assist businesses in locating information or assistance concerning the deregulation of telecommunications industries, the telephone industry, radio and television broadcasting, and cable television. It also assists in linking businesses to appropriate telecommunications contacts.

Contact: Office of Policy Analysis and Development, National Telecommunications and Information Administration, Department of Commerce, 14th & Constitution Avenue NW, Room 4725, Washington, DC 20230. Telephone (202) 482-1880; Fax (202) 482-1635. Web site: www.nt.a.doc.gov

Make Use of Federal Computerized Information Searches

Information searches tailored for your needs are obtainable from the Industrial Applications Centers. Two types of literature searches are available to you:

Retrospective Searches identify published or unpublished literature. Results are screened and documents identified according to a client's interest profile. Results are tailored to your specific needs. Backup reports identified in a search usually are available upon request.

Current Awareness Searches provide selected weekly, monthly, or quarterly abstracts on new developments in any selected area of interest. Companies will receive printouts automatically.

Technical assistance is also available. IAC engineers will help evaluate the results of these literature searches. They can find answers to technical problems and put clients in touch with scientists and engineers at appropriate NASA Field Centers.

You can obtain more information about these services by contacting your nearest center. User fees are charged for these information services. The addresses of the eight centers are:

Aerospace Research Applications Center, Indianapolis Center for Advanced Research, 611 N. Capitol Avenue, Indianapolis, IN 46204.

Kerr Industrial Applications Center, Southeastern Oklahoma State University, Station A, Box 2584, Durant, OK 74701.

NASA Industrial Applications Center, 823 William Pitt Union, University of Pittsburgh, Pittsburgh, PA 15260.

NASA Industrial Applications Center, University of Southern California, 3716 South Hope Street, Room 200, Los Angeles, CA 90007.

NASA-Florida State Technology Applications Center, University of Florida, 307 Weil Hall, Gainesville, FL 32611.

NASA/UK Technology Applications Program, University of Kentucky, 10 Kinkead Hall, Lexington, KY 40506.

NASA/RMS, P.O. Box 8757, BWI Airport, MD, 21090.

New England Research Applications Center, 1 Technology Drive, Tolland, CT 06084.

Questions About Standards, Specifications, Test Methods, and Nomenclature

The National Center for Standards and Certification Information maintains a reference collection on more than 240,000 standards, specifications, test methods, certification rules, codes, nomenclature, and recommended practices.

They can answer questions you may have such as:

- Are there standards for electric toasters?

- Have test methods been established for characteristics of bricks?

- Has nomenclature for quality control been defined?

- Have specifications for magnetic ink been established?

They can answer the same questions for some foreign countries, or can refer you to the right person.

A newsletter is published on proposed U.S. or foreign regulations that may affect U.S. manufacturers.

Contact: National Center for Standards and Certification Information, Room 2100, 100 Bureau Drive, National Institute of Standards and Technology (formerly Bureau of Standards), Gaithersburg, MD 20899. Telephone (301) 975-5507.

Sending Perishables Overseas

Most perishable agricultural commodities move into the export market by air or ocean transportation. Export Services assists you with ocean and airfreight transportation problems through a liaison with major transportation companies, shipping agencies, regulatory bodies, and foreign agricultural attaches.

If you encounter export problems, technical assistance and information is available to you. Specific information on the transportation requirements for exporting produce is available for you in two handbooks. Tip sheets on the transportation of livestock are available. In addition, reports on short-term applied research conducted on special problems encountered in the transport of agricultural products are available to you.

Contact: Export Services, Department of Agriculture, 14th & Independence Avenue SW, Washington, DC 20250. Telephone (202) 690-1304.

Help with Ocean Common Carriers

The Federal Maritime Commission provides a forum for settling disputes between carriers and shippers. The commission will listen to informal complaints and try to bring about a voluntary settlement. If warranted, formal proceedings can be initiated for unlawful practices. They may award reparations for economic injuries from violations. Each year they respond to over a thousand inquiries and complaints.

Contact: Office of Informal Complaints and Inquiries, Federal Maritime Commission, 800 N. Capitol Street NW, Washington, DC 20573. Speak with Bruce Dombrowski, Director, at (202) 523-5800, Fax (202) 523-3782.

Truck Costs and Technical Help

Many truckers of agricultural commodities are also small businessmen in that they use their own tractor/trailer rig to haul freight for a profit. For USDA refrigerator carriers, the Transportation Office publishes a monthly truck cost report, which provides information on current per-mile operating costs for a typical fresh fruit and vegetable trucker. Information on this report, as well as cost of trucking is available.

Contact: Truck Department, Agricultural Marketing Service, Department of Agriculture, 14th Street & Independence Avenue SW, Washington, DC 20250. Telephone (202) 690-1303.

Problems to Avoid If You're Starting a Trucking Company

The Public Service Office acts as a clearinghouse and focal point for the resolution of questions and problems experienced by businesses and individuals. It provides advice and technical assistance to small businesses, minority truckers, new entrants into the transportation field, small shippers, and small carriers, and deals with other members of the general public as well.

Its chief function is to counsel small business entities and individuals in understanding and coping with the rules, regulations, policies, and procedures of the commission. Much of this work involves assistance in obtaining operating rights—licenses to perform interstate transportation—from how to fill out the application form to complying with tariff filings and insurance requirements.

As part of its information outreach program, the office prepares and disseminates numerous booklets designed to answer your basic questions about the surface transportation industries. These include problems small businesses and individuals confront in entering the trucking business, starting a short-line railroad, and participating in rail abandonment proceedings.

The office plays a significant role in arming you for your product transportation challenges by initiating or commenting upon proposed rules or legislation relating to matters impacting upon areas of concern to your small business.

Contact: Surface Transportation Board, Department of Transportation, Washington, DC 20423. Telephone (202) 565-1668; Fax (202) 565-9003.

So You Want to Start a Small Railroad

It may surprise some to discover that the short-line railroad industry is experiencing a comeback. Each year, about two dozen new owners or operators are authorized to begin operation. One reason is the Department of Transportation's refusal to burden new operators with the cost of labor-protective conditions.

Write for a copy of *So You Want To Start a Small Railroad* from the Surface Transportation Board, Department of Transportation, Washington, DC 20423. Telephone (202) 565-1668; Fax (202) 565-9003.

CHAPTER 7

Financial Help

Financial Loans for Business in Small Towns

The U.S. Department of Agriculture's Business and Industrial Loan Program guarantees up to 90 percent of principal and interest on loans made by commercial lenders to establish or improve businesses and industries, if they are used primarily to help preserve or create new employment opportunities for rural people. Loans may assist enterprises located in the countryside and in towns or cities of up to a population of 50,000.

The money may be used for business acquisitions, construction, conversion, enlargement, repair, purchasing land, easements, buildings, equipment, and supplies. Some examples of recent businesses that received assistance are a radio station, cat fish farm, textile firm, and print shop.

The USDA has fewer rules than the SBA; for example, the USDA will consider loans for publishing enterprises and the SBA will (usually) not.

Business and Industrial Guaranteed Loans improve, develop or finance business, industry, and employment, and improve the economic and environmental climate in rural communities, including pollution abatement and control. This purpose is achieved through bolstering the existing private credit structure through guarantee of quality loans, which will provide lasting community benefits. This type of assistance is available to businesses located in areas outside any city with a population of 50,000 or more and its immediately adjacent urbanized or urbanizing area. Eligible entities include corporations, partnerships, cooperatives, federally recognized Indian tribes, individuals, and other legal entities.

Contact: U.S. Department of Agriculture, Rural Business Cooperative Service, 14th Street & Independence Avenue SW, Washington, DC 20250. Telephone (202) 690-0600; Fax (202) 690-4737; Web site: www.rurdev.usda.gov/agency/rbcds/html/bcdhome/htm

Loans for Teenagers

Rural Youth Loans from the U.S. Department of Agriculture are available to youngsters ages 10 through 20 in rural communities. The agency will finance nearly any kind of income-producing project. Kids have started landscaping companies, repair shops, catering services, roadside stands, and art/crafts sales enterprises, among others. The money may be used for equipment, supplies, renting tools, buying livestock, and for operating expenses. Only small projects are financed.

Contact: Rural Youth Loans, U.S. Department of Agriculture, Farm Service Agency, 12th St. & Independence Ave. SW, Washington, DC 20250. Telephone (202) 690-0600; Fax (202) 690-4737; Web site: www.rurdev.usda.gov/agency/rbeds/html/bcdhome/htm

Rural Enterprise Grants

Rural Business Enterprise Grants assist public bodies, nonprofit corporations, and federally recognized Indian tribal groups finance and facilitate development of small and emerging private business enterprises located in areas outside of a cities of 50,000 or more population. Funds may be used to finance and develop small and emerging private business enterprises. Costs that may be paid from grant funds include the acquisition and development of land and the construction of buildings, plants, equipment, access streets and roads, parking areas, utility, and service extensions; refinancing; fees for professional services; technical assistance and training associated with technical assistance; startup operating costs and working capital; providing financial assistance to a third party; production of television programs to provide information to rural residents; and creation, expansion, and operation of rural distance learning networks.

Contact: U.S. Department of Agriculture, 14th St. & Independence Ave. SW, Washington, DC 20250. Telephone (202) 720-1400; Fax (202) 690-0097.

Web site: www.rurdev.usda.gov/agency/rbeds/html/bcdhome/htm

Rural Development Grants

The purpose of Rural Technology and Cooperative Development Grants is to finance the establishment and operation of centers for rural technology and/or cooperative development. The grants are to improve the economic conditions of rural areas by promoting the development and commercialization of new services, products, processes, and enterprises in rural areas. Rural areas are areas outside the boundary of a city with a population of 50,000 or more and its immediately adjacent urbanized or urbanizing area. Eligible applicants are public bodies, nonprofit organizations, and federally recognized Indian tribal groups.

Contact: U.S. Department of Agriculture, 14th St. & Independence Ave. SW, Washington, DC 20250. Telephone (202) 720-3350; Fax (202) 720-4641.

Web site: www.rurdev.usda.gov/agency/rbeds/html/bcdhome/htm

More Rural Grants

The purpose of Rural Economic Development Loans and Grants is to finance rural economic development and rural job creation projects that are based on sound economic and financial analyses. Loans and grants are made to Rural Utilities Service (RUS) electric and telephone borrowers who use the funds to provide financing for business and community development projects. Loans are provided to finance a broad array of projects, including for-profit businesses. Grants are targeted to certain purposes such as community development assistance, education and training for economic development, medical care, telecommunications for education, job training or medical services, business incubators, and technical assistance. RUS borrowers may receive financing for grant purposes through either a grant to establish a revolving loan fund or a combination loan and grant.

Contact: U.S. Department of Agriculture, 14th Street & Independence Avenue SW, Washington, DC 20250. Telephone (202) 690-2583; Fax (202) 260-6494. Web site: www. rurdev.usda.gov/agency/rbcds/html/bcdhome/htm/

SBA's 504 Certified Development Company Program

The 504 Certified Development Company (CDC) Program provides growing businesses with long-term, fixed-rate financing for major fixed assets, such as land and buildings. A Certified Development Company is a nonprofit corporation set up to contribute to the economic development of its community or region. CDCs work with the SBA and private-sector lenders to provide financing to small businesses. There are about 290 CDCs nationwide. Each CDC covers a specific area.

Typically, a 504 project includes a loan secured with a senior lien from a private-sector lender covering up to 50 percent of the project cost, a loan secured with a junior lien from the CDC (a

100 percent SBA-guaranteed debenture) covering up to 40 percent of the cost, and a contribution of at least 10 percent equity from the small business being helped. The maximum SBA debenture generally is $750,000 (up to $1 million in some cases). The program is designed to enable small businesses to create and retain jobs; the CDC's portfolio must create or retain one job for every $35,000 provided by the SBA.

Proceeds from 504 loans must be used for fixed asset projects such as: purchasing land and improvements, including existing buildings, grading, street improvements, utilities, parking lots and landscaping; construction of new facilities, or modernizing, renovating or converting existing facilities; or purchasing long-term machinery and equipment.

The 504 Program may not be used for working capital or inventory, consolidating or repaying debt, or refinancing.

Interest rates on 504 loans are pegged to an increment above the current market rate for five-year and 10-year U.S. Treasury issues. Maturities of 10 and 20 years are available. Fees total approximately three percent of the debenture and may be financed with the loan.

Generally, the project assets being financed are used as collateral. Personal guaranties of the principal owners are also required.

Contact: Small Business Administration, Suite 800, 409 3rd Street SW, Washington, DC 20416. Telephone (202) 205-6481; Fax (202) 205-7722. Web site: www.sbaonline.sba.gov

7(a) Loan Guarantees

The 7(a) Loan Guaranty Program is one of SBA's primary lending programs. It provides loans to small businesses unable to secure financing on reasonable terms through normal lending channels. The program operates through private-sector lenders that provide loans that are, in turn, guaranteed by the SBA—the agency has no funds for direct lending or grants.

Most lenders are familiar with SBA loan programs so interested applicants should contact their local lender for further information and assistance in the SBA loan application process. Information on SBA loan programs, as well as the management counseling and training services offered by the agency, is also available from the local SBA office. For most SBA loans there is no legislated limit to the total amount of the loan that may be requested from the lender. However, the maximum amount the SBA can guaranty is generally $750,000. Thus, with a lender requesting the maximum SBA guaranty of 75 percent, the total loan amount available under this program generally would be limited to $1 million. However, there are some exceptions as presented below in the discussion of specialized loan programs.

Repayment ability from the cash flow of the business is a primary consideration in the SBA loan decision process but good character, management capability, collateral, and owner's equity contribution are also important considerations. All owners of 20 percent or more are required to personally guarantee SBA loans.

Contact: Small Business Administration, Suite 800, 409 3rd Street SW, Washington, DC 20416. Telephone (202) 205-6490; Fax (202) 205-7722. Web site: www.sbaonline.sba.gov

Certified Lenders

The most active and expert lenders qualify for the SBA's streamlined lending programs. Under these programs, lenders are delegated partial or full authority to approve loans, which results in faster service from SBA.

Certified lenders are those who have been heavily involved in regular SBA loan-guaranty processing and have met certain other criteria. They receive a partial delegation of authority and are given a three-day turnaround by the SBA on their applications (they may also use regular SBA loan processing). Certified lenders account for nearly a third of all SBA business loan guaranties.

Preferred lenders are chosen from among the SBA's best lenders and enjoy full delegation of lending authority in exchange for a lower rate of guaranty. This lending authority must be renewed at least every two years, and the SBA examines the lender's portfolio periodically. Preferred loans account for more than 10 percent of SBA loans.

Contact: Small Business Administration, Suite 800, 409 3rd Street SW, Washington, DC 20416. Telephone (202) 205-6481; Fax (202) 205-7722. Web site: www.sbaonline.sba.gov

A Fast Minimum Paperwork Loan

The Low Documentation Loan Program (LOWDOC) is a quick, one-page application, general-purpose loan guarantee program for $100,000 or less. The program requires the applicant have good credit and character. Personal guarantees of the principals are required.

The applicant completes the front side of a one-page application, the lending institution completes the back side, and the SBA gives you an answer in about five days.

Contact: Small Business Administration, Suite 800, 409 3rd Street SW, Washington, D.C. 20416. Telephone (202) 205-6481; Fax (202) 205-7722. Web site: www.sbaonline.sba.gov

General Information about the DELTA Loan Program

The Defense Loan and Technical Assistance Program (DELTA) is a joint effort between the SBA and the Department of Defense to provide financial and technical assistance to defense-dependent small firms adversely affected by cutbacks in defense. Each DELTA loan must achieve at least one of the following policy objectives: job retention—retain defense workers whose employment would otherwise be permanently or temporarily terminated due to defense reductions; job creation—create job opportunities and new economic activity in communities adversely affected by defense reductions; plant re-tooling and expansion—modernize or expand facilities in order to remain in the nation's technical and industrial base.

Contact: Small Business Administration, Suite 800, 409 3rd Street SW, Washington, DC 20416. Telephone (202) 205-6490; Fax (202) 205-7722. Web site: www.sbaonline.sba.gov/

General Information about the Qualified Employee Trusts Loan Program

The objective of this program is to provide financial assistance to Employee Stock Ownership Plans. The employee trust must be part of a plan sponsored by the employer company and qualified under regulations set by either the Internal Revenue Service Code (as an Employee Stock Ownership Plan or ESOP) or the Department of Labor (the Employee Retirement Income Security Act or ERISA). Applicants covered by the ERISA regulations must also secure an exemption from the Department of Labor regulations prohibiting certain loan transactions.

Contact: Small Business Administration, Suite 800, 409 3rd Street SW, Washington, DC 20416. Telephone (202) 205-6490; Fax (202) 205-7722. Web site: www.sbaonline.sba.gov/

General Information about the FA$TRAK Loan Program

The FA$TRAK Program is another SBA loan program designed to increase the capital available to businesses seeking loans of up to $100,000, but is currently offered as a pilot with a limited number of lenders. Under this program, certain lenders are authorized to use their existing documentation and procedures to make and service an SBA guaranteed loan. There are no additional forms and no waiting for SBA loan approval.

Contact: Small Business Administration, Suite 800, 409 3rd Street SW, Washington, DC 20416. Telephone (202) 205-6490; Fax (202) 205-7722; Web site: www.sbaonline.sba.gov

Small Business Investment Company Program

Congress created the Small Business Investment Company (SBIC) Program in 1958 to fill the gap between the availability of venture capital and the needs of small businesses in startup and growth situations. SBICs, licensed and regulated by the SBA, are privately owned and managed investment firms that use their own capital, plus funds borrowed at favorable rates with an SBA guarantee, to make venture capital investments in small businesses.

Virtually all SBICs are profit-motivated businesses. They provide equity capital, long-term loans, debt-equity investments, and management assistance to qualifying small businesses. Their incentive is the chance to share in the success of the small business as it grows and prospers.

There are two types of SBICs: regular SBICs and Specialized SBICs, also known as 301(d) SBICs. Specialized SBICs invest in small businesses owned by entrepreneurs who are socially or economically disadvantaged, mainly members of minority groups.

The program makes funding available to all types of manufacturing and service industries. Many investment companies seek out small businesses with new products or services because of the strong growth potential of such firms. Some SBICs specialize in the field in which their management has special knowledge or competency. Most, however, consider a wide variety of investment opportunities.

Contact: Small Business Administration, Suite 800, 409 3rd Street SW, Washington, DC 20416. Telephone (202) 205-6519; Fax (202) 205-6959; Web site: www.sbaonline.sba.gov

SBA's Microloan Program

The MicroLoan Program was developed to increase the availability of very small loans to prospective small business borrowers. Under this program, the SBA makes funds available to nonprofit intermediaries, who in turn make loans to eligible borrowers in amounts that range from under $100 to a maximum of $25,000. The average loan size is $10,000. Completed applications can usually be processed by the intermediary in less than one week.

Depending on the earnings of your business, the loan maturity may be as long as six years. Rates are pegged to no more than four percent over the prime rate. Fees are the same as for any 7(a) loan. Virtually all types of for-profit businesses that meet SBA eligibility requirements are eligible.

Each nonprofit lending organization has its own loan requirements, but must take as collateral any assets bought with the microloan. In most cases, the personal guaranties of the business owners are also required.

Contact: Small Business Administration, Suite 800, 409 3rd Street SW, Washington, DC 20416. Telephone (202) 205-6490; Fax (202) 205-7722; Web site: www.sbaonline.sba.gov

---

General Information about Short Term Loans and Revolving Lines of Credit

---

CAPLines is the umbrella program under which the SBA helps small businesses meet their short-term and cyclical working-capital needs. A CAPLines loan can be for any dollar amount (except for the Small Asset-Based Line described below).

There are five short-term working-capital loan programs for small businesses under the CAPLines umbrella:

Seasonal Line: These are advances against your anticipated inventory and accounts receivable help during peak seasons when businesses experience seasonal sales fluctuations. Can be revolving or non-revolving.

Contract Line: Finances your direct labor and material cost associated with performing assignable contract(s). Can be revolving or non-revolving.

Builder's Line: If you are a small general contractor or builder constructing or renovating commercial or residential buildings, this can finance direct labor and material costs. The building project serves as the collateral, and loans may be revolving or non-revolving.

Standard Asset-Based Line: This is an asset-based revolving line of credit for businesses unable to meet credit standards associated with long-term credit. It provides financing for cyclical growth, recurring and/or short-term needs. Repayment comes from converting short-term assets into cash, which is remitted to the lender. Businesses continually draw from this line of credit, based on existing assets, and repay as their cash cycle dictates. This line generally is used by businesses that provide credit to other businesses. Because these loans require continual servicing and monitoring of collateral, the lender may charge additional fees.

Small Asset-Based Line: This is an asset-based revolving line of credit of up to $200,000. It operates like a standard asset-based line except that some of the stricter servicing requirements are waived, providing that your business can consistently show repayment ability from cash flow for the full amount.

Contact: Small Business Administration, Suite 800, 409 3rd Street SW, Washington, DC 20416. Telephone (202) 205-6657; Fax (202) 205-7230. Web site: www.sbaonline.sba.gov

SBA's Surety Bond Program

By law, if you're a prime contractor to the federal government, you must post a surety bond on federal construction projects valued at $25,000 or more. Many state, county, city, and private-sector projects require bonding as well. The SBA can guarantee bid, performance, and payment bonds for contracts up to $1.25 million for small businesses that cannot obtain bonds through regular commercial channels. You may obtain your surety bonds by prior approval of the SBA or by applying through a surety-bonding agent.

Contact: Small Business Administration, Suite 800, 409 3rd Street SW, Washington, DC 20416. Telephone (202) 205-6540; Fax (202) 205-7230. Web site: www.sbaonline.sba.gov

Loan Guarantees for Agricultural Exports

The Export Credit Guarantee Program (GSM-102) run by the Agriculture Department's Commodity Credit Corporation is designed to expand U.S. agricultural exports by stimulating U.S. bank financing of foreign purchases on credit terms of up to three years. In every transaction, the foreign buyer's bank must issue an irrevocable letter of credit covering the port value of the commodity exported.

The Credit Corporation's guarantee will cover most of the amount owed to the U.S. bank in case the foreign bank defaults. The program operates in situations where credit is necessary to increase or maintain U.S. exports to a foreign market and where private financial institutions would be unwilling to provide financing without guarantee.

A secondary objective is to permit some countries with improved financial conditions to purchase on fully commercial terms.

The Intermediate Export Credit Guarantee Program (GSM-103) is similar but provides you with coverage on credit terms in excess of three but not greater than ten years.

Under these programs, your guarantee coverage may be made available to you on credits extended for freight cost and marine and war risk insurance costs associated with U.S. agricultural exports. The Credit Corporation announces availability of such coverage on a case-by-case basis.

Contact: Foreign Agricultural Service, Commodity Credit Corporation, Department of Agriculture, P.O. Box 2415, Washington, DC 20013. Telephone (202) 720-4274; Fax (202) 690-0727; Web site: www.usda.gov.fas

Grants for Inventions

The Energy-Related Inventions Office encourages innovation in non-nuclear energy technology by helping individual inventors and small R&D companies to develop promising energy-related inventions. It evaluates all submitted inventions and recommends those that are promising.

The evaluation criteria that your invention must meet are: technical feasibility, degree of energy impact, commercial potential, and intrinsic technical merit. The Department of Energy (DOE) then reviews your recommended inventions and, working closely with you, determines the next reasonable step for the invention and how much money it will take. Most often, support takes the form of a one-time-only cash grant and technical assistance in developing linkages with the private sector.

Contact: Innovative Concepts Program, U.S. Department of Energy, 1000 Independence Avenue SW, Washington DC 20585. Telephone (202) 586-0139 or (202) 586-9232.

Funds for Fishing

The Commercial Fisheries Financial Assistance Programs include the:

- Fisheries Obligation Guarantee Program, which provides a federal guarantee of financing of commercial fishing vessels and shoreside facilities.

- Capital Construction Fund Program, which defers federal income taxes for agreement holders on commercial fishing operations to permit accumulation of capital for use in, approved commercial fishing vessel acquisition or reconstruction projects.

Contact: National Oceanic and Atmospheric Administration, National Marine Fisheries Service, Department of Commerce, Financial Services Division, F/TWI 1315 East West Highway, Silver Spring, MD 20910. Telephone (301) 713-2390. Fax (301) 713-2258.

If Your Fishing Boat or Gear is Destroyed

If your fishing boat is destroyed by a foreign vessel or if your fishing gear is damaged by an oil-related activity, the government may make direct payments to you from one of the following programs:

Boat Destruction—The applicant must be a U.S. commercial fisherman and a U.S. citizen. The incident must have occurred within the U.S. Fishery Conservation Zone or in an area where the United States has exclusive management authority.

Gear Loss—If you lost gear because of an oil- or gas-related activity in any area of the outer Continental Shelf, the government will pay for the gear plus 50 percent of the resulting economic loss.

Approximately 150 claims per year are paid for gear damage, ranging from $500 to $25,000.

There are no restrictions on the use of these funds.

For both of the above programs, you must present financial statements, receipts, log books, and affidavits to establish that you are a fisherman and owned the equipment for which compensation is claimed.

Contact: Financial Services Division, Attn: National Marine Fisheries Service, Department of Commerce, 1315 East West Highway, Silver Spring, MD 20910. Telephone (301) 713-2390; Fax (301) 713-2258.

If Your Fishing Boat Is Seized

The Department of State will reimburse you if a foreign country seizes your fishing boat on the high seas.

In addition, if your boat was seized in waters claimed by the foreign country as territorial, but the United States does not recognize the claim, the State Department will still pay.

Pro-registration and payment of a premium fee are necessary.

Losses payable are limited to the market value of the fish before seizure, market value of the boat and gear, and 50 percent of the gross income lost.

Each year claims totaling about $1,600,000 are paid. Whether or not you pre-register, the government will reimburse you for fines paid to a foreign government to secure the release of your boat.

Contact: Office of Fisheries, Bureau of Oceans and International Environment, Room 5806, Dept. of State, Washington, DC 20520-7818. Telephone (202) 647-3262; Fax (202) 647-1106.

Minority Loans for Department of Energy Research

The Minority Loan Program was established to assist minority business enterprises in participating fully in DOE research, development, demonstration, and contract activities. The financial assistance is in the form of direct loans, whereby DOE will provide funds to a minority business borrower from its appropriated funds.

The loans are to assist a minority business borrower in financing up to 75 percent of costs a borrower incurs in preparing a bid or proposal to attempt to obtain DOE contracts or agreements.

The maximum amount of money that can be borrowed for any one loan is $50,000.

Contact: Minority Economic Impact Office, Dept. of Energy, 1000 Independence Ave. SW, Room 5B-110, Washington, DC 20585. Telephone (202) 586-7377 or (202) 586-0888.

Financing of Foreign Architectural and Engineering Projects

The Export-Import Bank (Eximbank) provides financing to help U.S. architectural and engineering firms win foreign contracts for project-related feasibility studies and pre-construction engineering services. Under the program, Eximbank, the U.S. Government agency charged with facilitating financing for U.S. exports, offers medium-term loans directly to the foreign purchasers of those services, and guarantees private financing for a portion of the local costs of the project.

To qualify for the program, the contract must involve a project with the potential to generate additional U.S. exports worth $10,000,000 or twice the amount of the initial contract, whichever is greater.

Contact: Export-Import Bank of the United States, 811 Vermont Avenue NW, Washington, DC 20571. Telephone (800) 565-3946 or (202) 565-3904; Fax (202) 565-3931; Web site: www.exim.gov

Insurance on Credit to Foreigners

American companies often find that extending credit to foreign buyers is essential to expand or win business. But distance, unfamiliar legal procedures and unforeseen political or economic events make credit sales to foreign buyers riskier than similar sales to domestic customers.

Eximbank's Policies, offered through its agent, the Foreign Credit Insurance Association (FCIA), makes it easier for companies, even those with little or no exporting experience, to get credit risk protection for their export credit sales.

Four policies are offered:

The Umbrella Policy enables state and local government agencies, banks, export trading companies, freight forwarders and other financial and professional organizations to become administrators of short-term credit risk insurance covering the export sales of numerous exporters. These administrators assume responsibility for collecting premiums, reporting shipments, filling out forms, and processing claims on behalf of the exporters insured under their Umbrella Policy.

This policy gives new exporters greater access to foreign credit risk protection and lessens their paperwork burdens. It also helps exporters get financing because the policy proceeds are assignable to any financial institution as collateral on a hold harmless basis. Administrators of Umbrella Policies benefit as well. The Umbrella

Policy enables them to offer an important service to their small- and medium-sized business customers.

The New-to-Export Policy assists companies that are just beginning to export or have an annual export sales volume of less than $750,000.

The Short-Term Multi-Buyer Policy is available for any exporter.

The Bank-to-Bank Letter of Credit Policy is available to any bank financing export sales on an irrevocable letter of credit basis.

Products and services include consumables, raw materials, spare parts, agricultural commodities, capital goods, consumer durables, and services.

Contact: Export-Import Bank of the United States, 811 Vermont Avenue NW, Washington, DC 20571. Telephone (800) 424-5201; firms in Alaska, Hawaii and Washington, DC, should call (202) 565-3649; Fax (202) 565-3675. Web site: www.exim.gov

Fixed Rate Loans for Exports

Eximbank offers a wide range of financial support programs, including loans and guarantees of loans made by others. The loan and guarantee programs cover up to 90 percent of the U.S. export value, with repayment on each transaction it supports. Creditworthiness of the buyer, the buyer's country, and the exporter's ability to perform are considered.

Eximbank's loans provide competitive, fixed interest rate financing for U.S. export sales facing foreign competition backed by subsidized financing from another government. Evidence of such competition is not required for exports produced by small businesses where the loan amount is $2,500,000 or less.

Eximbank extends direct loans to foreign buyers of U.S. exports and intermediary loans to fund responsible parties who agree to lend to foreign buyers. Eximbank's interest rates follow the guidelines of the export credit arrangement among members of the Organization for Economic Cooperation and Development.

Eximbank's guarantees provide repayment protection for private sector loans to creditworthy foreign buyers of U.S. goods and services. Eximbank's guarantees are available alone or may be combined with an intermediary loan. Most guarantees provide comprehensive protection for both political and commercial risks.

Contact: Export-Import Bank of the United States, 811 Vermont Avenue NW, Washington, DC 20571. Telephone (800) 424-5201; firms in Alaska, Hawaii, and Washington, DC, should call (202) 565-3904; Fax (202) 565-3931.

International Trade Loan Program

The International Trade Loan Program helps small businesses that are engaged in or preparing to engage in international trade, as well as those adversely affected by competition from imports, to acquire or modernize facilities or equipment that will be used in the production of goods or services within the United States. SBA can guarantee up to $1,000,000 for facilities or equipment and $250,000 for working capital.

Contact the SBA district office nearest you, or the U.S. Small Business Administration, Office of International Trade, 409 Third Street, SW, Washington, DC 20416. Telephone (202) 205-6720; Fax (202) 205-7230.

More Loan Guarantees, Including Insurance for Exporters

The Overseas Private Investment Corporation (a government agency) offers the Contractors and Exporters Program to improve the competitive position of American contractors and exporters seeking to do business in the developing nations. OPIC offers specialized insurance and financing services.

Many developing countries require foreign firms to post bid, performance or advance payment guarantees in the form of standby letters of credit when bidding on or performing overseas contracts. OPIC's political risk insurance for contractors and exporters protects against the arbitrary or unfair drawing of such letters of credit.

In addition, contractors and exporters may obtain insurance against the risks of:

- currency inconvertibility
- confiscation of tangible assets and bank accounts
- war, revolution, insurrection, and civil strife
- losses sustained when a government owner fails to settle a dispute in accordance with the provisions of the underlying contract

OPIC also offers a special loan guaranty program for small business contractors to assist with their credit needs. This plan provides an OPIC guaranty of up to 75 percent of a stand-by letter of credit that is issued to a financial institution on behalf of a small-business contractor.

Contact: Overseas Private Investment Corporation, 1100 New York Avenue NW, Washington, DC 20528. Telephone (800) 424-6742; for businesses within Washington, DC, call (202) 336-8457; Fax (202) 408-9862.

Working Capital Guarantees for Exporters

Exporting is an important opportunity for many American companies. Sometimes, however, small and medium sized businesses have trouble obtaining the working capital they need to produce and market goods and services for sale abroad.

Despite their creditworthiness, these potential exporters find commercial banks and other lenders reluctant to offer them working capital financing. Some companies have already reached the borrowing limits set for them by their banks.

Others do not have the type or amount of collateral their banks require. That's why the Export-Import Bank of the United States developed the program. Eximbank does not lend to exporters directly. Instead, it encourages commercial banks and other lenders to make working capital loans by guaranteeing that, in the event of default by the exporter, Eximbank will repay most of the loan.

For more details, ask for the Working Capital Guarantee Program.

Contact: Export-Import Bank of the United States, 811 Vermont Avenue NW, Washington, DC 20571. Telephone (800) 424-5201; firms in Alaska, Hawaii, and Washington, DC, should call (202) 565-3904; Fax (202) 565-3931; Web site: www.exim.gov

---

Money and Insurance for Investing in Overseas Ventures

American investors planning to share significantly in the equity and management of an overseas venture can often utilize OPIC's finance programs for medium-to-long-term financing.

To obtain OPIC financing, the venture must be commercially and financially sound, within the demonstrated competence of the proposed management, and sponsored by an investor having a proven record of success in the same or closely related business.

OPIC's financing commitment of a new venture may extend to, but not exceed, 50 percent of the total project cost. A larger participation may be considered for an expansion of a successful, existing enterprise.

Currently, OPIC provides financing to investors through two major programs. Direct loans, which are available only for ventures sponsored by, or significantly involving, U.S. small businesses or cooperatives, and loan guarantees, which are available to all businesses regardless of size.

OPIC will issue you a guaranty under which funding can be obtained from a variety of U.S. financial institutions. The guaranty covers both commercial and political risks.

While private investors generally have the capability to assess the commercial aspects of doing business overseas, they may be hesitant to undertake long-term investments abroad, given the political uncertainties of many developing nations. To alleviate these uncertainties, OPIC insures U.S. investments against three major types of political risks.

Inconvertibility coverage protects an investor against the inability to convert into U.S. dollars the local currency received as profits, earnings, or return of capital on an investment. OPIC's inconvertibility coverage also protects against adverse discriminatory exchange rates.

Expropriation coverage protects the investor not only against classic nationalization of enterprises or the taking of property, but also a variety of situations that might be described as 'creeping expropriation.'

Bellicose-Action Coverage is provided against political violence for loss due to war, revolution, insurrection, and politically motivated civil strife.

Contact: Overseas Private Investment Corporation, 1100 New York Avenue NW, Washington, DC 20528. Telephone (800) 424-6742; for businesses within Washington, DC, call (202) 336-8597; Fax (202) 408-5142.

Loans for the Handicapped and for Veterans

Handicapped people and Vietnam veterans unable to obtain financing in the private credit marketplace may be eligible, first, for a guaranteed/insured loan or, alternatively, for a direct loan if no bank will participate in a guaranteed loan. These loans may be used to construct, expand, or convert facilities; to purchase building equipment or materials; or to provide working capital.

The borrower must meet the SBA's definition of a small business. The applicant must:

- be of good character
- show an ability to operate a business successfully
- have a significant stake in the business
- show that the business can operate on a sound financial basis

You must be prepared to provide a statement of personal history, personal financial statements, company financial statements, and summary of collateral. Your loan must be of such sound value or so secured as to provide reasonable assurance of repayment.

You generally file your application in the SBA field office serving the territory where your business is located. Approval takes thirty to sixty days from the date of the application acceptance, depending on the type of loan. The applicant is notified by an authorization letter from the district SBA office or participating bank.

Contact: The Office of Financial Assistance, Small Business Administration, Room 804, 409 3rd Street SW, Washington, DC 20416. Telephone (202) 205-6774; Fax (202) 205-6903; Web site: www.sbaonline.sba.gov

Money for Small Business Innovative Research

All federal departments at one time or another have research money and contracts available for small business participants in this process. Pre-solicitation announcements are available periodically from the SBA. Check your nearest SBA office for dates and details. Usually a three-month lead is given between the announcement and the time a solicitation proposal must be submitted.

In accepting a federal contract, be mindful of the fact that you must reply to the exact specifications required, exhibit the ability to perform according to your bid and/or contract, and have to have the fiscal liquidity to wait for payment until the responsible federal department unravels the inevitable red tape. While delays and bureaucratic nit picking are not commonplace or intended, they can happen; however, if you can produce according to the exacting specifications, doing business with the world's largest customer can be mighty profitable.

Departments that most frequently participate in SBIR solicitations include the U.S. Departments of Commerce, Defense, Energy, Health & Human Services, and the Environmental Protection Agency.

Typical SBIR programs include:

- drinking water treatment
- municipal and industrial wastewater treatment and pollution control
- biological sludge treatment for improved handling and disposal
- solid and hazardous waste disposal
- treatment of hazardous and toxic waste at Superfund sites
- innovative restoration technologies removing heavy metals at Superfund sites
- control of acid rain precursors
- process instrumentation for improved pollution control
- waste reduction and pollution prevention
- oil spill prevention, cleanup and restoration technology
- improved measurement technologies for lead detection in lead-based paints.

Requirements are changed frequently and new ones are added. You should remember that all measurement indicated in proposals and projects must be in the metric system.

The 10 departments that have permanent SBIR representatives who can be consulted for particulars are the following:

Department of Agriculture
Director, SBIR Program
U.S. Department of Agriculture
Room 323-J, Aerospace Building
901 D Street, SW
Washington, DC 20250-2200
(202) 401-4002 or Fax (202) 401-3541

Department of Commerce
Director, Office of Small and Disadvantaged Business
    Utilization
U.S. Department of Commerce
14th and Constitution Ave., NW HCHB, Room 6411
Washington, DC 20230
(202) 482-1472

Department of Defense
SBIR Program Manager OSD/SADBU
U.S. Dept. of Defense the Pentagon Room 2A340
Washington, DC 20301-3061
(703) 614-1151

Airforce (703) 697-4126
Army (703) 697-7753
Navy (703) 602-2695

Department of Education
SBIR Program Coordinator
U.S. Department of Education Room 602F
555 New Jersey Avenue, NW Washington, DC 20208
(202) 708-9820

Department of Health And Human Services
SBIR Program Manager, Office of the Secretary
U.S. Department of Health and Human Services
Washington, DC 20201
(202) 690-7300

Department of Transportation
Chief, University Research
Technology Innovation and Programs Office (DTS-22)
U.S. Department of Transportation
Research and Special Programs Administration
Volpe National Transportation Systems Center
Kendall Square
Cambridge, MA 02141-1093
617) 494-2224 or Fax (617) 494-2370

Environmental Protection Agency
SBIR Program Manager
Research Grants Staff (RD-675)
Office of Research and Development
Environmental Protection Agency
401 M Street, SW Washington, DC 20460
(202) 564-5315 or Fax (202) 565-2469

National Aeronautics and Space Administration
Program Director, SBIR Price-Code CR
National Aeronautics and Space Administration Hdqtrs.
Washington, DC 20546
(202) 358-2088 or Fax (202) 358-3261

National Science Foundation
SBIR Program Managers
National Science Foundation
4201 Wilson Blvd.
Arlington, VA 22230
(703) 306-1330

Nuclear Regulatory Commission
SBIR Program Representative

Program management
Policy Development and Analysis Staff
U.S. Nuclear Regulatory Commission
Rockville, MD 20852
(301) 415-7380

Assistance in Obtaining Capital for Small Business Innovative Research Awardees

A system is available to identify potential sources of capital that may help SBIR awardees commercialize their research and development activities. This system is a free service that provides a roster of potential investors such as venture capitalists, corporations, and state government programs.

The database is searchable by technology and industry areas, thereby allowing the office to identify the sources of capital most likely to be interested in a particular company.

This system was also designed to assist SBIR awardees seeking PhaseII awards, which require that special consideration be given to proposals demonstrating PhaseIII non-federal capital commitments.

Contact: Innovation, Research, and Technology Office, Small Business Administration, 409 3rd Street SW, Room 500, Washington, DC 20416. Telephone (202) 205-6365; Fax (202) 205-7754.

Grants for Broadcasting Stations

The Public Telecommunications Facilities Program provides grants to assist in the planning and construction of public telecommunications facilities. Special emphasis is placed on extending public broadcasting signals to currently unserved areas.

Construction grants are awarded as matching grants up to 75 percent of the total cost. Planning grants are awarded up to 100 percent of the funds necessary for planning a project.

Special consideration is given to women and minorities.

Contact: Public Telecommunications Facilities Program, National Telecommunications and Information Administration, U.S. Department of Commerce, Washington, DC 20230. Telephone (202) 482-5802.

Money for Pollution Control

Your business may be eligible for pollution control financing if your are unable to obtain private financing on terms or at rates comparable to businesses that do not fit the SBA definition of a small business.

Your loan proceeds may be used for aspects of constructing and placing into operation any eligible facility that the SBA determines is likely to prevent, reduce, abate, or control noise, air, or water pollution.

SBA offers you several options for the kinds of financing instruments that can be used. Lenders can also generate funds for your loans by using marketable securities such as taxable bonds and debentures within authorized loan limits. The principal is not to exceed $5,000,000.

Contact: Small Business Administration, Pollution Control Financing Staff, 409 3rd Street SW, Washington, DC 20416. Telephone (202) 205-6365; Fax (202) 205-7754.

Equity Loans

Equity investments and long-term loans are available to you from small business investment companies (SBICs) and section 301(d) small business investment companies (301(d)s), which are privately-owned firms licensed by the SBA and partly funded by the federal government.

256 SBICs are located throughout the U.S., many of which are assisted or "leveraged" by the U.S. Small Business Administration. 133 other SBICs are licensed to provide assistance to small businesses owned by socially- or economically disadvantaged persons.

Some SBICs seek out small businesses with new products or services because of the strong growth potential of such firms.

Some SBICs have management skilled in specific industries and focus on them in their financing.

According to SBA criteria, for your firm to be eligible for SBIC financing, it must have a net worth of under $6,000,000 and a net after-tax income during the previous two years of $2,000,000 or less. To determine the size of your business, the SBA must consider all affiliated operations of your company.

Your application for SBIC financing requires a minimum two-step process:

1. Identify a SBIC that will handle your type of financing, and

2. Prepare a current business plan or prospectus that includes the following seven items:

  • Identification, product or service
  • product facilities and property
  • marketing plan
  • competition
  • management and references

- financial statements
- a statement of the benefits you hope to gain from the financing.

A directory of SBICs is available from your nearest SBA office.

Your loan must be of at least five years maturity and interest rates, which are subject to negotiation, may not exceed current ceiling. SBICs and 301(d)s generally emphasize income-generating investments, such as convertible debentures and straight long-term debt. SBICs tend to be most active in providing growth capital to established businesses, and are active in financing high technology, start-up enterprises.

You should prepare a business plan that describes your enterprise's operations, financial condition, and financing, including information on your products, new product lines, patent positions, market and competitive data, sales and distribution, key personnel, and other pertinent factors.

Your nearest SCORE office can be of help in preparing the proper business plan. See the section on SCORE, the Service Corps of Retired Executives. Note that Section 301 (d). SBICs finance only socially or economically disadvantaged small business.

Contact: Small Business Administration, Capital Access, 409 3rd St. SW, Washington, DC 20416. Telephone (202) 205-6657; Fax (202) 205-7230.

Save Money on Taxes, Become a Foreign Sales Corporation

A Foreign Sales Corporation (FSC) is a corporation that obtains an exemption on corporate taxes on a portion of the profits earned on exports or services. Usually 15 percent of the profits are tax-free.

There are "regular" FSCs and small FSCs; small FSCs' rules are easier for you to cope with.

You can obtain a brochure on the rules and some applications by phoning (202) 482-3277, or write the Office of Trade Finance, U.S. Department of Commerce, International Trade Administration, Washington, DC 20230.

Starting a Federal Credit Union

The National Credit Union Administration will explain how you can get started, help prepare the charter application, assist in startup operations, and provide depositor insurance.

For established credit unions in low-income communities, they also have direct loans.

The guideline for eligibility is that you can start a credit union if you have an association with at least 3000 potential members, although smaller groups with sponsorship may apply.

For more information, ask for the Credit Union Information Package. Contact: National Credit Union Administration, 1775 Duke Street, Alexandria, VA 22313. Telephone (703) 518-6440; Fax (703) 518-6319.

Economic Injury Disaster Loans

The Disaster Assistance Division of the Small Business Administration can help you if your business concern suffers economic injury as a result of natural disasters. If your business was within the disaster area, see the next entry, Physical Disaster Loans.

100,000 of these loans are made annually. Your terms are up to thirty years for repayment with a $1,500,000 limit.

The funds are for paying current liabilities, which the small concern could have paid if the disaster had not occurred. Working capital for a limited period can be provided to continue operations until conditions return to normal.

For more information you should request the pamphlet titled *Economic Injury Disaster Loans for Small Business.*

Contact: Disaster Assistance Div., Small Business Administration, 409 3rd Street SW, Washington, DC 20416. Telephone (202) 205-6734; Fax (202) 205-7728.

Physical Disaster Loans

The Disaster Assistance Division of the Small Business Administration can help you if your business is physically damaged by a natural disaster such as a hurricane, flood, or tornado. If your business is not physically damaged, but suffers economically, see the preceding section, Economic Injury Disaster Loans.

50,000 loans are made annually totaling $1,100,000,000. In general the terms are for thirty years, with a limit of $500,000, although if high unemployment will result, the amount can be higher. The SBA will establish an on-site office to help with processing and disbursement.

For more information you should request the pamphlet titled *Physical Disaster Loans.*

Contact: Disaster Assistance Division, Small Business Administration, 409 3rd Street SW, Washington, DC 20416. Telephone (202) 205-6734; Fax (202) 205-7728.

Start a Small Airline

If you'd like to provide air services to small towns, the Department of Transportation (DOT) may be able to help. The DOT subsidizes service to approximately 150 communities that would otherwise not have air access. The payments cover costs and return needs. The annual payments range from $80,000 to $850,000 per destination.

Contact: Director, Office of Aviation Analysis, P-S0, Department of Transportation, 400 Seventh Street SW, Washington, DC 20590. Telephone (202) 366-1061; Fax (202) 366-7638.

Flood Insurance

The Federal Insurance Administration enables you or your small business to purchase insurance against losses from physical damage to buildings and their contents. The premium rate is generally lower than a normal actuarial rate, reflecting a subsidy by the federal government. Your maximum coverage is $250,000 for your small business structures and $300,000 for the contents.

The FIA has a large selection of booklets available for you that explain the program, design guidelines for reducing floor damage, how to understand flood insurance rate maps, etc.

Contact: Federal Insurance Administration, FEMA, Washington, DC 20472. Speak with Harriette Kinberg at (202) 646-3431; Fax (202) 646-7970.

Wrestling with Tax Matters

The "Your Business Tax Kit" was developed for presentation to operators of new businesses as they are formed. Its purpose is to encourage more effective voluntary compliance by helping new

117

businesspersons become fully aware of their responsibilities for filing all the federal tax returns for which they may be liable and for paying the taxes due.

The kit is an envelope designed to hold your forms and instructions for preparing most business tax returns.

You may pick up your kit at an IRS office or you may request that it be mailed to you.

Small Business Tax Workshops are conducted regularly throughout the country. For more information or to request a publication, call (800) 424-1040.

Emergency Loans for Farmers and Ranchers

The U.S. Department of Agriculture has loans to assist family farmers, ranchers, and agriculture operators to cover losses suffered from major disasters. You may use your loan to repair, restore or replace your damaged property and supplies and, under some circumstances, to refinance your debts.

Your maximum loan is $500,000; your interest rate is 3.75 percent.

Contact: U.S. Department of Agriculture, Washington, DC 20250. Telephone (202) 720-1764.

Loans for Non-Profit Corporations

The U.S. Department of Agriculture has loans, loan guarantees, and grants to rural development and finance corporations that improve business, industry and employment in rural areas through the stimulation of private investment and foundation contributions.

The non-profit corporation may serve profit or nonprofit businesses but they must be local. The corporation must be authorized to do business in at least three states.

For more information, contact: Administrator, Farm Service Agency, Department of Agriculture, Washington, DC 20250. Telephone (202) 720-9223; Fax (202) 720-8261.

Small Forest Projects

If you own 1,000 acres or less of forest land capable of producing industrial wood crops, the Forestry Incentives Program may be of interest to you. The government will share up to 65 percent of the cost of tree planting, timber stand improvement, and site preparation. $12,000,000 is provided annually.

Contact: Conservation and Environmental Protection Division, Department of Agriculture, P.O. Box 96060, Washington, DC 20090. Telephone (202) 205-1697; Fax (202) 205-1012.

Money for Ships

The Department of Transportation Maritime Administration will provide you with loan guarantees to promote your construction of ships for foreign and domestic commerce.

Your vessel(s) must be designed for research or for commercial use in coastal or intercoastal trade, on the Great Lakes, on bays, rivers, and lakes of the U.S., in foreign trade, or as floating drydocks. Any ship not less than five net tons (other than a towboat, barge, scow, lighter, canal boat or tank vessel of less than 25 gross tons) is eligible.

The ship owner must provide 25 percent of the total cost. These guarantees have been used to build large ships such as tankers, ocean-going liners, dredges, jack-up drilling rigs, and container ships. Numerous smaller ships including ocean-going and inland tugs and barges have also been funded.

Contact: Associate Administrator, Maritime Administration, Department of Transportation, Washington, DC 20590. Telephone (202) 366-5802; Fax (202) 366-3889.

Mortgage Insurance

If you rent housing to low or middle income, the elderly, in urban renewal areas, or are a credit risk because of low income, the Department of Housing and Urban Development may be able to assist you by providing mortgage insurance.

Contact: Insurance Division, Office of Insured Multifamily Housing Development, Department of Housing and Urban Development, Washington, DC 20410. Telephone (202) 708-2700.

Grants, Grants, and More Grants

The following are examples of grants being given by the federal government. Since these come and go, it is essential for you to check for up-to-date information with each department.

National Endowment for the Arts
1100 Pennsylvania Avenue NW
Washington, DC 20506
(202) 682-5441; Fax (202) 682-5660

- document preservation
- dance companies
- film/video of art of dance
- art services
- experimental initiatives
- traditional art
- folk art
- innovative art
- writers and translators

- literary distribution
- literary magazines
- small press assistance
- residencies for writers
- audience development narrative
- film development
- radio production
- radio workshops
- museum services
- museum projects
- music presentations
- music festivals
- jazz projects
- music ensembles
- choruses
- composers
- creative orchestra
- solo recitalists
- music recording
- theater works
- regional touring
- mime
- producers
- theater training
- playwrights
- visual artists
- art education
- translations
- humanities
- preservation of newspapers

Federal Emergency Management Agency
500 C Street NW
Washington, DC 20472
(202) 646-2500

- emergency broadcast systems

Department of Justice
Bureau of Prisons
320 First Street Room 200
Washington, DC 20534
(202) 307-3230; Fax (202) 514-9481

- improvement of corrections programs
- research of criminal behavior
- training of corrections staff
- juvenile crime research

Bureau of Land Management
Department of Interior
1849 C Street NW
Washington, DC 20240
(202) 208-6731; Fax (202) 208-5242

- management of public lands
- grants program

Department of Housing and Urban Development
451 7th Street NW
Washington, DC 20416
(202) 401-6367; Fax (202) 401-8939.

- neighborhood rehabilitation

Department of Energy
1000 Independence Avenue SW
Forrestal Building Room 5B-110
Washington, DC 20585
(202) 586-5575

- energy research
- fossil energy
- nuclear energy
- renewable energy
- coal technology
- basic energy research

Economic Development Administration
Department of Commerce Room H-7317
14th and Constitution Avenue
Washington, DC 20230
(202) 482-4067; Fax (202) 273-4781

- chronic economic depression
- economic development

Office of Vocational and Adult Education
Department of Education
400 Maryland Avenue SW Room 519
Washington, DC 20202
(202) 708-8270; Fax (202) 205-8973

- adult education
- bilingual instruction
- foreign language studies
- Indian and Hawaiian native education

Department of Health and Human Services
200 Independence Avenue SW
Washington, DC 20201
(202) 690-7300

- dentistry
- developmental disabilities
- nursing research
- nursing training
- population research
- aging research
- international biomedical exchanges
- mental health research
- alcohol abuse
- biophysics and physiological sciences clinical research
- retinal and choroidal research
- anterior segment research
- microbiology and infectious diseases research
- immunology

- kidney disease
- diabetes research
- lung research
- heart research
- arthritis research
- cancer research
- AIDS research
- animal research

Environmental Protection Agency
401 M Street NW
Grants Administration Division PM 216
Washington, DC 20460
(202) 564-4100

- solid waste disposal
- hazardous waste disposal
- air pollution research
- pesticides control

Department of Interior
12201 Sunrise Valley Drive
Geological Survey MS 424 National Center
Reston, VA 22092
(703) 648-7313.; Fax (703) 648-5070

- water resources research

National Oceanic and Atmospheric Administration
1305 East West Hwy.
Silver Springs, MD 20910
(310) 713-0926

- climate and atmospheric research
- marine research
- Soil Conservation Office

Department of Agriculture
P.O. Box 2890
Washington, DC 20250
(202) 720-0127; Fax (202) 720-4390

- abandoned mine program
- agricultural research

National Science Foundation
4201 Wilson Blvd
Arlington, VA 22210
(703) 306-1210

- scientific, technological and international affairs
- biological, behavioral and social studies
- biosciences
- mathematical and physical sciences
- engineering research

Some Money-Raising Hints to Get to Uncle Sam & Others

You probably think first and foremost of the Small Business Administration (SBA) for Uncle Sam handouts. True, billions of dollars have been dispensed by this agency, but it's equally true that much of this was never repaid and getting new business bucks today is not always easy.

The SBA will consider a loan or loan guaranty only if two commercial banking sources have denied you credit. However, while a bank might lend you money for five to seven years, the SBA can help extend the loan over ten years—thus spreading out the payback and helping your cash flow.

The SBA is more favorably inclined toward minorities.

The SBA will lend money in distressed areas, while most banks will not.

The SBA may lend you money with a lower credit rating than a bank would require, although the SBA will probably insist on personal guaranties (such as collateral on your home), while a bank might be satisfied with only commercial guaranties.

The SBA will back a less-than-$100,000 loan called a "LowDoc" loan that banks have accepted eagerly since mid-1994. It cuts a lot of red tape and you generally get approval in one to three weeks.

The SBA is not your only source of government loans. The federal government offers you about a thousand different loan programs through virtually all of its departments. Ask the SBA.

If you buy a business, you might have to pay "key money"; have this subjective portion of the purchase price included in the total (paying the seller only $1 for goodwill or a non-compete clause) and get a loan on the total amount-in this way you can probably borrow 100 percent of the purchase price and save your own cash for operating the business.

Remember that seller-financing beats SBA or bank financing.

Remember also the cynic's advice—that the best number to know is the telephone number of a rich relative.

When making any kind of loan, remember the "three Cs" and prepare them carefully in advance of your application: **credit, cash flow, collateral**. If you cannot satisfactorily answer the "three-C" requirements, keep your day job.

Don't overlook your own and your immediate family's fiscal resources. These might surprise you. The more you can gather together from your personal resources, the less you need to borrow and the less you need to pay back. It also makes your personal statement look better and easier to get more money from the SBA or banks. Financial people know that if you're willing to share in the risk, they are less likely to say "no."

What to Do if the Government Won't Give You a Loan

A different approach to owning a successful business avoids loans from institutions. A brief outline of the technique goes as follows:

- Many new businesses fail, so avoid this obstacle by buying a proven successful business.

- All businesses are for sale. The next time you go into a business that looks prosperous and interesting to you, ask who the owner is. If he's on the premises, go into his office; if not, phone him from the nearest phone booth. Ask him, "Have you ever considered selling this business." The answer is always "yes." Tell him you're interested. Plan on seeing him a number of times for informal discussions.

- The owner will ask you, "How much can you put down?" Reply that the amount put down depends on the financial status of the company, but that you'll need some owner financing. Usually he or she will say that if you will put 20 to 30 percent down, he'll provide financing. Be sure to ask for twenty- to thirty-year financing. Don't worry about not having the down payment in hand. (See last paragraph.)

- Make sure the company makes a good profit; it's easier for you to purchase a company that produces $200,000 to $300,000 a year profit than it is for you to purchase one that makes only $10,000 a year profit. Besides going through the books, talk to his suppliers. A supplier can often tell you if a business is profitable, and can usually give you insight into its reputation.

- Is the company run by a manager? Has he been there for more than five years? If so, ask him if he'll stay if you buy the business.

- Who are the suppliers? Contact them and ask them what they think about the prospective business. **If they are** enthused and their reports are favorable, tell them you want to buy the business and will need some "working capital" (this is your down payment but you should never call it that). You may need to grant concessions such as the exclusive rights to supply you. There are a large variety of interbusiness financial agreements. Usually one will fit your purposes. This is the largest source of business loans in the U.S. today.

That's your approach in a nutshell. You can create many variations of the theme. There are a number of seminars that teach this basic method. Watch for one in your area.

CHAPTER 8

International Trade

The Trade Information Center

The Trade Information Center (TIC) publishes a comprehensive description of export assistance programs from 19 federal agencies. It's available to you in electronic format or hard copy. To receive one, you can call 1-800-USA-TRADE (in real numbers, that's 1-800-872-8723).

The TIC has numerous other trade publications available to you by fax-on-demand. Call the above number from the headset of your fax machine. Trade specialists at the TIC can help you to find out:

- how you can start an import/export business

- how you can determine if your company is "export-ready"

- where you can get information on importing

- how you can get market information on a specific country

- where you can find "New-to-Export" seminars

- how you can get government help on advertising overseas

- where you can locate trade leads

- if you need an export license

- if there's a tariff or quota on your product in a particular country
- where you can find export financing
- what you can do about unfair treatment by foreign governments or firms

The Trade Information Center is located in the U.S. Dept. of Commerce, 14th and Constitution Ave. NW, Washington, DC 20230. Telephone (800) 872-8723; fax (202) 482-4473

Export Counseling and Financial Assistance

The International Trade Office facilitates financial assistance and other appropriate management and technical assistance to small business concerns that have the potential to become successful exporters. The program provides basic export counseling and training, which includes:

- one-on-one counseling by SCORE volunteers with significant international trade expertise
- access to university research and counseling
- assistance from professional international trade management consulting firms
- referral to other public or private sector expertise
- initial consultation with an international trade attorney of the Federal Bar Association
- business management training
- international trade and export marketing publications

Contact: International Trade Office, Small Business Administration, 409 3rd Street SW, 8th Floor, Washington, DC 20416. Telephone (202) 205-6720; Fax (202) 205-7230. Web site: www.sbaonline.sba.gov

Export Seminars

The Bureau of Export Administration's seminar staff teaches exporters about the national security requirements for international sales. U.S. exporters and foreign importers of American products around the world increase their knowledge and understanding of U.S. Export Regulations by attending classroom instruction offered by the export seminar staff. The Export Administration Regulations Course is a professional seminar featuring two or three days of classroom training on export controls and licensing procedures.

Seminars are held in major cities throughout the United States and in foreign countries. Both introductory and advanced courses on the Export Administration Regulations are offered. Completing the introductory course is a prerequisite for receiving advanced instruction.

The seminars assist a business in understanding the requirements for compliance with U.S. export laws and procedures, to improve its ability to use and understand federal export regulations, to prepare better license applications and other documentation, to find out how a company can avoid the costly fines and time-consuming seizures that result from violation of export laws, and to discover ways to increase productivity, ease license application efforts, and lower costs of doing business abroad.

These seminars have proven valuable to manufacturers, carriers, shipping agents, freight forwarders, international sales and marketing specialists, contracts administrators, materials and traffic managers, customer service representatives, buyers, accountants, attorneys, freight forwarders, technical supervisors, order processors, and export licensing coordinators.

Contact: Bureau of Export Administration, Department of Commerce, 14th & Constitution Avenue NW, HCHB Room 1099D, Washington, DC 20230. Telephone (202) 482-6031 or (202) 482-0436; Fax (202) 482-3322.

Export Management and Marketing Help for Smaller Businesses

The Agency for International Development (AID), implements the U.S. Foreign Economic Assistance Program in more than 80 countries throughout Africa, Europe, Near East, Asia, Latin America, and the Caribbean. The Office of Small and Disadvantaged Business Utilization offers counseling services and marketing assistance to U.S. firms interested in exporting goods, and technical assistance through AID-financed projects.

AID participates in two set-aside programs: the SBA 8(a) program, and the Small Business Set-aside program. Unique to AID is the Gray Amendment which requires that 10% of prime contracts be set aside for socially and economically disadvantaged businesses, women-owned businesses, historically Black Colleges and Universities, U.S. colleges and universities with at least 40 percent enrollment of Hispanic American students and minority-controlled private voluntary organizations.

The Office maintains the AID Consultant Registry Information System (ACRIS), an automated database identifying U.S. businesses and their areas of expertise.

As legislatively mandated and for the benefit of U.S. businesses, AID publishes, free of charge, procurement information bulletins advertising intended procurement of AID financed commodities (goods, products, material). To subscribe to the bulletins, request a mailing list application from OSDBU.

You may obtain these notices free of charge by completing the mailing list application.

Contact: Agency for International Development, Room 1400-A, SA-14, Washington, DC 20523-1414. Telephone (202) 712-1500; Web site: www.web.fie.com/web/fed/aid

Overseas Promotion of Your Product

The International Trade Administration's Export Promotion Services will assist exporters through a variety of programs and services that analyze foreign markets, locate buyers and representatives overseas, and promote products and services. In addition, they offer export-counseling services for all aspects of the export process. International trade experts are located worldwide in 66 U.S. cities and 127 overseas cities.

Trade Fairs are shop windows in which thousands of firms from many countries display their wares. These fairs are international marketplaces in which buyers and sellers can meet conveniently.

A Trade Fair Certification Program advises and assists sponsors of these fairs in promoting the events; gives the fairs official Department of Commerce recognition, and counsels exhibitors. In addition, official U.S. participation is sponsored in key international trade fairs in all parts of the world.

Three types of trade missions have been developed to help U.S. exporters penetrate overseas markets. Specialized trade missions bring groups of U.S. business people into direct contact with potential foreign buyers, agents, and distributors.

Seminar missions promote sales of sophisticated products and technology in markets where sales can be achieved more effectively by presenting technical seminars or concentrating on concepts and systems. They feature one- and two-day presentations by a team of U.S. industry representatives who conduct discussions on the technology of their industry.

Trade associations, chambers of commerce, state development agencies, and similar groups with the advice and support of the agency organize industry-Organized Government-Approved (IOGA) trade missions.

In addition to product exhibitions, the Overseas Export Development Office facilities are available to trade associations and to individual firms or their agents for Business-Sponsored Promotions (BSPs). BSPs may include sales meetings, conferences, or seminars. Finally, catalog exhibitions and video/catalog exhibitions are low-cost, flexible kinds of exhibitions that can provide U.S. industry with an effective technique to give products exposure overseas, test the salability of the products, develop sales leads, and identify potential buyers, agents or distributors.

Both are held at U.S. Embassies or Consulates or in conjunction with trade shows. These two kinds of exhibitions are especially useful in promoting U.S. exports in remote and small markets of the world where major equipment exhibitions are not feasible.

Contact: International Trade Administration, United States and Foreign Commercial Service, Department of Commerce, Export Promotion Services, 14th & Constitution Avenue NW, Room 2116H, Washington, DC 20230. Telephone (202) 482-6220; Fax (202) 482-2526. Web site: www.doc/gov/resources/ITA_info. html

Applying for an Export License

The Bureau of Export Administration (BEA) offers you several services to assist in the licensing process. This office is the bureau's licensing customer service unit, staffed with licensing information experts. It helps to solve or answer your questions about how to apply for an export license. These experts can help you prepare license applications and guide you through export regulations.

In developing an export strategy, companies need to review the U.S. export laws as they relate to a planned export. For reasons of national security, export of certain technologies is controlled through two types of export licenses: general and validated.

The BEA should be called when you have a specific question about export regulations or current policy, need license information on overseas trade fairs, have an emergency license request that may need special handling, or want to find out your licensing case number.

Electronic License Application Information Network (ELAIN) allows on-line computer acceptance of export license applications for all free world destinations. ELAIN offers U.S. exporters a fast and convenient way to submit or receive license applications. After receiving applications, the office processes, reviews, and issues the license electronically. Applications may cover all commodities except super-computers.

First, exporters apply for authorization to submit applications electronically by writing to the BEA's address to the attention of ELAIN. The exporter should provide the name and address of the applicant company, a phone number, and the name of the contact person.

The Office of Exporting Licensing will provide information on how to obtain company identification numbers and personal identification numbers to individuals approved by the office and the exporting company to submit license applications. The exporter will also receive instructions on how to contact the CompuServe computer network to obtain detailed filing instructions.

Once you and other exporters have the necessary authorization to begin submitting license applications electronically to ELAIN, you will be able to enter license-related information into your own personal computer and send it to the Commerce Department via e-mail. Licensing decisions in turn will be electronically conveyed back to you.

They'll help you get export licensing publications and forms, the most important of which is Export Administration Regulations.

Since the Bureau of Export Administration receives between 500 and 600 applications every day, it's important for you to obtain these information publications early in the marketing stage so that you fully understand the export-licensing program.

To subscribe to the Export Administration Regulations contact the Superintendent of Documents, U.S. GPO, Washington, DC 20402. Telephone (202) 512-1800. Reference subscription number 903-012-00000-5.

Exporters may obtain forms required by the bureau by calling the Exporter Assistance staff at (202) 482-4811 or writing Bureau of Export Administration, Department of Commerce, P.O. Box 273, Washington, DC 20044. Attn: forms.

STELA (System for Tracking Export License Applications) is a computer-generated voice unit that interfaces with the Department of Commerce ECASS (Export Control Automated Support System) database. It provides accurate and timely information on the status of license applications.

STELA tells an exporter exactly where an application is in the system and for how long it has been there. It can also give an exporter authority to ship his or her goods for those applications approved without conditions. Exporters still receive a hard copy of the license by mail, but an exporter can ship with STELA's approval before receiving it.

Exporters with a touch-tone phone can call STELA at (202) 482-2752; it will answer "Hello, I'm STELA, the Department of Commerce export license system. Please enter your license application number or hang up." Using the push buttons on the phone, enter the license application number. Following the entry, in synthesized voice response, STELA gives the status of the case. If you need to talk to a person about STELA, call (202) 482-2572.

STELA can also handle questions about the amendment applications. After announcing the status of one case, STELA prompts the caller to enter another case number or hang up. STELA is in operation weekdays from 7:15 a.m. to 11:15 p.m. EST and on Saturdays from 8:00 a.m. to 4:00 p.m. The database is updated each night, so you should check your application's status once a day.

Contact: Bureau of Export Administration, Department of Commerce, 14th & Constitution Avenue NW, HCHB Room 1099D, Washington, DC 20230. Telephone (202) 482-0064; Fax (202) 482-3322. Web site: www.doc.gov/resources/BXA_info. html

How to Find New Opportunities in Foreign Markets

Competition in the world market is becoming ever more challenging and foreign governments have increased support for their exporters. The Export Trading Company Act of 1982 offers U.S. business new opportunities to compete in foreign markets. The goal of this legislation is to encourage the development of American Export Trading Companies (ETC), particularly for the benefit of small and medium-sized companies.

This office promotes and encourages the formation of ETCs, counsels firms interested in exporting, provides a contact facilitation service between U.S. producers and firms providing export trade services, administers the Title III Antitrust Certificate of Review Program, and conducts ETC conferences.

Contact: The Export Trading Company Affairs, International Trade Administration, Trade Development, Department of Commerce, 14th & Constitution Avenue NW, Washington, DC 20230. Telephone (202) 482-5131; Fax (202) 482-1790; Web site: www.doc.gov/resources/BXA_info.html

Identifying and Evaluating Overseas Markets

The new Commercial Information Management System (CIMS) electronically links all the economic and marketing information of ITA trade specialists and offices worldwide, allowing vital business data to be delivered on a timely basis. Custom-tailored market research information packages are available on:

- foreign business and economic climate
- import regulations
- tariff and non-tariff barriers
- domestic and foreign competition
- individual competitor firms and competitive factors
- distribution practices
- how products are promoted in the market
- policies
- product standards
- end users

In addition, CIMS can provide information on; foreign agents, distributors, importers, manufacturers, retailers, government purchasing officials, and end users interested in your product or service type. CIMS can provide, tailored to your specifications:

- names of contacts
- telex FAX, cable, and phone numbers
- product or service specialties
- year established
- number of employees
- relative size of firms

Contact: Information and Research Services Office, International Trade Administration, United States and Foreign Commercial Service, Department of Commerce, 14th & Constitution Avenue NW, Washington, DC 20230. Telephone (202) 482-5281; Fax (202) 482-2526

Lists of Overseas Customers and Companies

The Export Information Systems (XIS) Data Reports provides lists of the largest markets and competition sources for a company's products.

XIS is an export/import data bank of trade information of approximately 2,500 product categories showing their performance in the world market. This information is based on Standard International Trade Classification (SITC) statistics supplied by the United Nations. XIS produces two kinds of reports:

- **Product Reports** give information on the top 35 import markets for a product and on the top 25 world markets for U.S. exporters, based on the percentage of market share and dollar sales volume.

- **Country Reports** give information on the top 20 products imported into a specific country, the top 10 U.S. products imported into the country, by market share and the top 10 U.S. products imported into the country, by sales volume.

Contact: Dept. of Commerce, U.S. & Foreign Commercial Service Information Systems Office, 14th & Constitution Ave. NW, Washington, DC 20230. Telephone (202) 482-5291; Fax (202) 482-5862. Web site: www/doc.gov

Advertising to 100,000 Foreign Executives, Distributors and Government Officials

Commercial News USA promotes U.S. products and services available for export to more than 100,000 overseas agents, distributors, government officials, and end-users. Additional distribution is made of selected products and services through reprints in local media.

Commercial News USA contains descriptions of 150 to 200 products, services, and trade and technical literature with black and white photographs in each issue. In addition to featuring general new products, all issues highlight individual industries and receive special promotion by U.S. commercial officers overseas at industry trade events.

While much depends on the product being promoted, firms typically average thirty to forty inquiries each and initial sales averaging over $10,000. There is a fee for you to advertise in the magazine.

Contact: Associated Business Publications International, Commercial News USA, 317 Madison Avenue, Suite 1900, New York, NY 10017. Telephone (212) 490-3999; Fax (212) 822-2028.

Trade Leads on Overseas Sales Opportunities for Agricultural-Related Products

The AgExport Connections Trade Lead Service provides continual access to timely sales leads from overseas firms seeking to buy or represent American food and agricultural products. Businesses have a direct pipeline to trade leads gathered by Foreign Agricultural Service (FAS) offices worldwide.

Both new and established American exporters can use trade leads as a fundamental sales tool, which brings foreign buyers' purchasing needs directly to them.

Each day, FAS agricultural counselors, attachés, and trade officers around the world locate and develop trade opportunities. They find sales opportunities with foreign companies, government purchasing agencies, brokers, distributors, and others, and determine information needed to pursue each trade lead-product specifications such as labeling and packaging, quantities, end uses, delivery deadlines, bid requirements, e-mail contact points, and mailing addresses. These trade leads are then forwarded to AgExport within hours, and distributed.

Leads are available the same day to U.S. exporters through a number of commercial computerized information networks. Trade leads also can be mailed daily to clients in the United States who have subscribed to a special mail service.

A bulletin is available, which includes all trade leads processed each week. It is mailed weekly and is targeted toward export agents, trade associations, and companies interested in export opportunities for a wide variety of food and agricultural products.

The bulletin also highlights upcoming trade shows, foreign trade developments, and changes and updates in trade policy. Specialists can also generate various mailing lists of prospective buyers for you.

Contact: Foreign Agricultural Service, Department of Agriculture, AgExport, 14th & Independence Avenue SW, Room 4639-S, Washington, DC 20250. Telephone (202) 720-6343; Fax (202) 690-0193. Web site: www.usda.gov/fas

Help for Food Exporters

The Label Clearance Program (LCP) was designed to help U.S. food processors and exporters locate foreign markets and sales opportunities for U.S. commodities new to overseas markets.

Although many of these products have long since been tested and accepted by American customers, the products have not been marketed in many foreign countries.

Each participating U.S. firm is provided with information on the foreign countries' requirements for imported foods. Without this information the job of exporting to a foreign market can be costly and time-consuming.

The LCP review can answer such questions as: where must the country of origin appear on the label; in what order must the product ingredients be listed; what is the required language and are bilingual labels or stick-ons acceptable, et al.

The LCP office conducts a screening of each company's label and product information to ensure completeness before it is submitted for overseas evaluation. Once this screening is completed the information is forwarded to LCP review in the targeted country.

The final product specific report prepared by an overseas post contains a brief statement on the product's marketability in the specific overseas country. This objective assessment of the product's ability to compete in the targeted market is provided to assist the U.S. firm in its evaluation of the product's competitiveness.

A new part of the LCP Services is the Country Product Clearance Summary. This report provides the participating company with a concise statement on the taste and eating habits of the country, information on the legal requirements and standards that govern the packaging and labeling of imported foods, and the business customs of the targeted country.

Summary reports for Japan, Mexico, Germany, Switzerland and France have been completed.

Contact: The Label Clearance Program, Foreign Agricultural Service, Department of Agriculture, High Value Products Division, 14th & Independence Avenue SW, Room 4649-S, Washington, DC 20250. Telephone (202) 720-7115; Fax (202) 690-1727; Web site: www.usda.gov/fas

Advertising Your Agricultural Products Overseas

A monthly newsletter, Contacts for U.S. Agricultural Products, can assist you by introducing your food or agricultural products to foreign markets. It is sent to Foreign Agricultural Service counselors, attachès, and trade officers for distribution to prospective foreign buyers. It is translated into Japanese, Spanish, French, Italian, and Greek and mailed to thousands of buyers worldwide. Brief, 100-word descriptions of products submitted by U.S. firms are published each month.

Contact: Foreign Agricultural Service, Department of Agriculture, Agricultural Information and Marketing Service, 14th & Independence Avenue SW, Room 4649-S, Washington, DC 20250. Telephone (202) 690-1148; Fax (202) 690-0193. Web site: www.usda.gov/fas

When an Export Licensing Emergency Occurs

A business may have an emergency requiring immediate attention. In justifiable emergencies, generally when the situation is out of the applicant's control, the applicant or his authorized agent should contact this office or the nearest district office to expedite handling of an application.

The validity of a license issued under this special processing procedure expires no later than the last day of the month following the month of issuance. Because a company is expected to use a license issued on an emergency basis immediately, the Office of Export Licensing will not extend the validity period of a license.

Contact: Bureau of Export Administration, Office of Export Licensing, Department of Commerce, 14th & Pennsylvania Avenue NW, HCHB Room 1099D, Washington, DC 20230. Telephone (202) 482-0062; Fax (202) 482-3322.

When You Need Technical Answers for Products Under Export Control

At the request of exporters, advisory options and classification determinations are issued on commodities to be exported from the United States.

The Export Counseling Office is responsible for establishing export control policy under the authority of the Export Administration Act.

It develops, in association with other U.S. agencies and the International Coordinating Committee (COCOM), export control and decontrol proposals. It analyzes and develops national security, foreign policy, and short supply control programs; revises and develops implementing Export Administration Regulations, and reviews and resolves technical and policy issues related to export applications and appeals of licensing determinations.

Contact: Export Counseling Office, Bureau of Export Administration, Department of Commerce, 14th & Constitution Avenue NW, HCHB Room 4069A, Washington, DC 20230. Telephone (202) 482-4811; Fax (202) 482-3322

Locating Overseas Representatives for Your Firm

A unique program provides custom overseas searches for interested and qualified foreign representatives on behalf of a U.S. client.

U.S. commercial officers abroad conduct the search on a single country and prepare a report identifying up to six foreign prospects that have personally examined the U.S. firm's product literature and have expressed interest in representing the firm.

Contact: Agent/Distributor Service (ADS), International Trade Administration, United States and Foreign Commercial Service,

Department of Commerce, Washington, DC 20230. Telephone (202) 482-0692; Fax (202) 482-2526

National Trade Data Bank

The National Trade Data Bank (NTDB) provides a comprehensive source of international trade and export data from 17 federal agencies, including the Foreign Trade Index, which is an extensive list of foreign companies interested in establishing trade links with U.S. companies. The NTDB contains over 105,000 documents, related monthly and available on CD-ROM by subscription.

Contact: Trade Development, 14th & Constitution Avenue NW, Washington, DC 20230. Telephone (202) 482-5281; Fax 482-2526

Economic Bulletin Board

The Economic Bulletin Board (EBB) provides an on-line computer service accessible by computer. You can download available economic and trade news, official press releases, and statistical data prepared by a wide range of federal agencies. Files are continually updated. Annual subscriptions are available.

Contact: Trade Development, 14th & Constitution Avenue NW, Washington DC 20230. Telephone (202) 482-5281; Fax 482-2526. To try EBB as a guest user with your personal computer, call (202) 482-3870.

Eastern Europe Business Information Center

The center is stocked with a wide range of publications on doing business in Eastern Europe; these include lists of potential partners, investment regulations, priority industry sectors, and notices of upcoming seminars, conferences, and trade promotion events. It also serves as a referral point for programs of voluntary assistance to the region.

Contact: Eastern Europe Business Information Center. Telephone (202) 482-1599; Fax (202) 482-3159

To Reach an Export Specialist for a Specific Country

Where should a U.S. exporter go to find out about agent/distributor agreements in Saudi Arabia? About how to recover a business debt resulting from Mexico's foreign exchange crisis? About Canada's investment approval process? About a trade show in Germany? About countertrade with Tanzania? About tariff rates in Paraguay?

The best sources of information on such matters are country desk officers who can handle such questions and provide other useful commercial information as well.

These specialists perform a unique service. They look at the needs of the individual U.S. firm wishing to sell in a particular country in the full context of that country's overall economy, trade policies and political situation, and also in the light of U.S. policies toward the country.

Desk officers keep up to date on the economic and commercial conditions in their assigned countries. Each collects information on the country's regulations, tariffs, business practices, and economic and political developments, including trade data and trends, and market size and growth that affect ability to do business. Each keeps tabs on the country's potential as a market for U.S. products and services and for U.S. investment.

Call (202) 482-2000 or (202) 482-3022 and ask for the export specialist for the country you're interested in. Fax (202) 482-5444. Or write them at: Country Export Specialists, International Trade

Administration, International Economic Policy, Department of Commerce, 14th & Constitution Avenue NW, Room 3864, Washington, DC 20230.

Export Management and Networking Assistance Near You

Businesses help promote and assist in increasing U.S. exports through the International Trade Administration's District Export Councils. The councils work to enlist the efforts of the American business community to help government expand export opportunities and increase U.S. exports abroad.

There are 51 councils with 1800 members representing every state and territory of the United States. They have an increased role in the development of U.S. trade policy. Organized work plans are developed by each council to carry out initiatives locally to promote exporting.

The councils have become a vital multiplier in export awareness and promotion, and represent a local voice in the establishment of trade policies. Firms interested in contacting their local councils should call this office.

Contact: District Export Councils, International Trade Administration, United States and Foreign Commercial Service, Dept. of Commerce, 14th & Constitution Avenue NW, Washington, DC 20230. Telephone (202) 482-4811 or (800) 872-8723.

Where You Can Get Trade Data, Competitive Assessments, and Analysis Data

The Trade Information and Analysis Program monitors and provides you with trade data, conducts macro-economic trade research and analysis, assesses U.S. industrial competitiveness, and operates an Office of Trade Finance, which offers you counseling on offset/countertrade practices to U.S. exporters.

The program also produces a series of publications, such as *Industrial Outlook, Competitive Assessments, Trade Performance,* and *U.S. Foreign Trade Highlights.*

Industrial Outlook, published annually, features assessments and forecasts of business conditions for more than 350 industries. You may obtain a copy at any Government Printing Office for $24.

Competitive Assessments are periodic reports that assess the medium- and long-range competitiveness of specific U.S. industries in international trade.

Some recent titles include *Cement, Automobile, Materials Handling Equipment, Sporting Goods, Cellular Radio Equipment, International Construction, Computer Systems, Civil Helicopters,* and *Fiber Optics.* You can obtain each of these at any Government Printing Office at a cost between $3 and $7.

The Trade Performance series, published annually, provides you with a detailed analytical look at the U.S. trade performance and positions.

The *U.S. Foreign Trade Highlights,* published annually, details trade data trends in U.S. foreign trade in selected regions and with major trading partners. The current issue is available at any Government Printing Office.

Contact a Government Printing Office or International Trade Administration, Trade Development, Department of Commerce, 14th & Constitution Avenue NW, Washington, DC 20230. Telephone (202) 482-5487; Fax (202) 482-4821

Sales Leads from Overseas Firms

The Trade Opportunities Program (TOP) provides timely sales leads, joint ventures, and licensing opportunities from overseas firms and foreign governments seeking to buy or represent U.S.

products and services. U.S. Commercial Officers worldwide gather leads through local channels.

Lead details, such as specifications, quantities, end-use, delivery, and bid deadlines, are delivered daily to Washington, and then made available electronically within 24 hours directly to the U.S. business community in both printed and electronic form through private sector nationwide distributors.

To contact the Economic Bulletin Board for electronic distribution call (202) 482-1986 or Fax (202) 482-2164. To try EBB as a guest user with your computer call (202) 482-3870. Both new and established exporters can use TOP as a fundamental sales tool.

Contact: Trade Opportunities Program (TOP), International Trade Administration, United States and Foreign Commercial Service, Department of Commerce, 14th & Constitution Avenue NW, Washington, DC 20230. Telephone (800) 872-8723. Web site: www.doc/gov/resources/ITA_info.html

Credit and Other Info on Foreign Firms

Two sources of background information on foreign firms are the World Traders Data Reports and the Eximbank.

The World Traders Data Reports (WTDRs) are provided on individual foreign firms, containing information about each firm's business activities, its standing in the local business community, its credit-worthiness, and its overall reliability and suitability as a trade contract for U.S. exporters.

WTDRs are designed to help U.S. firms locate and evaluate potential foreign customers before making a business commitment.

A typical WTDR includes: name, address, and key contact, number of employees, type of business, general reputation in trade and financial circles, an assessment of the firm's suitability as a trade contact, year established, sales territory, and products handled.

Compiled by U.S. Commercial Officers abroad, WTDRs reflect their knowledge of local firms and business practices and include an evaluation of a company's suitability as a trade contract. In addition to normal checks with banks, trade and financial references, corporate and public records, local credit agencies and customers, the embassy uses its own files and contacts to compile each report.

In many less-developed countries, where even routine commercial information can be hard to get, WTDRs offer an excellent alternative to the difficult and painstaking task of acquiring information through individual contacts.

Contact: WTDRs, International Trade Administration, United States and Foreign Commercial Service, Department of Commerce, 14th & Constitution Avenue NW, Washington, DC 20230. Telephone (202) 482-5281 or (800) 872-8723

Credit Information on Foreign Firms

Credit information of exceptional value is also available from the Eximbank to the commercial banking community and U.S. exporting firms in the financing of export sales to a specific country or individual company abroad.

To date, this has been one of the many resources of the Export-Import Bank that has not been utilized to full advantage. In keeping with traditional business practices, Eximbank will not divulge confidential financial data on foreign buyers to whom it has extended credit, nor will it disclose classified or confidential information regarding particular credits or conditions in foreign countries. However, the experience as related to repayment records of companies or countries with which Eximbank has done business can have a definite bearing on a decision to pursue certain export transactions overseas.

In addition, Eximbank is in a position to obtain additional information through its association with the banking and exporting community and other international agencies whose reviews might be helpful in determining if the export-financing project should be undertaken.

The principal targets in Eximbank's campaign to furnish good credit data are the smaller exporters and commercial banks with limited international trade facilities.

Contact: Export-Import Bank of the United States, 811 Vermont Avenue NW, Washington, DC 20571. Telephone (202) 565-3946.

Information on Fisheries in Foreign Countries

The Foreign Fisheries Analysis Program monitors marine fisheries around the world. It collects, evaluates, and distributes information on the latest political, economic, and scientific developments in world fisheries that affects the U.S. fishing industry or U.S. Government policies and programs.

The division also provides information concerning international shrimp and salmon aquaculture developments.

Contact: National Oceanic and Atmospheric Administration, National Marine Fisheries Service, Department of Commerce, 1335 East-West Highway, Silver Spring, MD-20910. Telephone (202) 713-2328.

Domestic and Foreign Fisheries Market News

The Market News Program offers current information on prices, market conditions, landings, imports, exports, cold-storage holdings, and market receipts of fishery products.

Information is collected by market reporters, and compiled and disseminated by Market News offices in Boston, New York, New

Orleans, Terminal Island, and Seattle. The information aids U.S. buyers and sellers of fishery products in making intelligent marketing decisions.

Also reported is ancillary information such as innovations in harvesting, production, marketing, packaging and storage of fishery products, federal fishery regulations and legislation, Regional Fishery Management Council meetings and activities, foreign fishing activities, foreign market information, and fishery meetings.

Contact: Market News Program, National Oceanic and Atmospheric Administration, National Marine Fisheries Service, Dept. of Commerce, 1315 East-West Highway, Silver Spring, MD 20910. Telephone (301) 713-2239; Fax (202) 713-2258.

Counseling on Bi-National Technical Joint Ventures

Information and counseling is available for those interested in establishing bi-national technology-oriented joint ventures. Experience with the successful U.S.-Israeli bi-national Industrial Research and Development Program is used as the basis. The service focuses on higher technology and smaller businesses which have little knowledge of how to expand into operations abroad.

Contact: International Operations, Office of Technology Commercialization, Department of Commerce, Building 820, Route 270, Gaithersburg, MD 20899. Telephone (301) 975-3084.

Legal Assistance on Duty Refunds

Refund assistance in the form of drawback is a provision of law by which a lawfully collected duty or tax is refunded or remitted, wholly or partially, because of a particular use made of the commodity on which the duty or tax was collected.

It encourages U.S. exporters by permitting them to compete in foreign markets without the handicap of including in the sales price the duty paid on the imported merchandise.

Since the exporter must know, before making contractual commitments, that he or she will be entitled to drawback on the exports, the drawback procedure is designed to give exporters this assurance and protection.

Drawback is payable to the exporter unless the manufacturer reserves the right to claim the refund. Several types of drawback are authorized under 19 U.S.C. 1313.

For more information, ask for the pamphlet Drawback, A Duty Refund on Certain Exports from any Government Printing Office bookstore or from the office below.

Contact: Entry Rulings Branch, U.S. Customs, Department of the Treasury, 1301 Constitution Avenue NW, Washington, DC 20229. Telephone (202) 927-2320; Fax (202) 927-1876.

Free Legal Consultations for Exporters

Under an agreement with the Federal Bar Association, exporters with questions about international trade can receive free, initial legal consultation with an experienced trade attorney under the Export Legal Assistance Program (ELAN). Local, private attorneys around the country volunteer their time to assist small business exporters. Questions that can be addressed include:

- selling overseas
- getting paid
- licensing agreements
- joint ventures
- export regulations
- domestic and foreign taxation
- dispute resolution

Contact your local SBA district office or ELAN attorney listed on the following Web site: www.miep.org/elan/ Or contact Judd L. Kessler, National Coordinator Export Legal Assistance Network, 1667 K Street NW, Washington, DC 20006. Telephone (202) 778-3080.

If You've Been Hurt by Unfair Foreign Trade Practice

The Trade Remedy Assistance Office provides you with information on remedies and benefits available under trade laws and on the procedures necessary to obtain these benefits. For example, if you produce an item in competition with an item being imported and imports are increasing as to be a substantial cause of serious economic injury to the domestic market, a tariff adjustment or import quota may be imposed.

Affected firms and workers can also apply for financial assistance.

If a foreign government is subsidizing a product, you can petition for a countervailing duty to be imposed on the product.

If a foreign company is selling merchandise at less than fair value (dumping) in the U.S., anti-dumping duties may be imposed. Also technical assistance and informal legal advice is provided.

Contact: Trade Remedy Assistance Office, International Trade Commission, 500 E Street SW, Room 317, Washington, DC 20436. Telephone (202) 205-2200.

Investment Opportunities Overseas

Two programs run by the Overseas Private Investment Corporation (a government agency) are the Investor Information Service and the Opportunity Bank.

If you're an American businessperson considering an overseas venture, obtaining basic information about foreign countries and their business environments is your critical first step.

Unfortunately, this is frequently a difficult and time-consuming process, given the variety of potential information sources and the resulting research required.

Investor Information Service

To assist U.S. firms in gathering such information, as well as facilitate the flow of information about developing countries to potential U.S. investors, OPIC has created the Investor Information Service (IIS). IIS is a publication clearinghouse that provides interested companies and individuals with easy one-stop shopping for basic data and information commonly sought when considering investment overseas.

The materials, which are assembled into kit form, have been obtained from various U.S. government agencies, foreign governments and international organizations. Together these source materials cover the economies, trade laws, business regulations and attitudes, political conditions, and investment incentives of specific developing countries and areas.

The information kits packaged by IIS are categorized by individual countries as well as major geographic regions and are sold for a nominal fee. At present, IIS kits are available for more than 110 developing countries and 16 regions.

Opportunity Bank

A major stumbling block in the Third World's attempt to attract U.S. investment capital arises from the limited flow of information between potential U.S. equity investors and likely sponsors of investment projects in the developing countries. In its continuing effort to promote U.S. direct investment in the developing nations, OPIC has sought to establish channels of investment information by developing a computerized data system called the Opportunity Bank.

The primary purpose of this data bank is to enable U.S. firms and overseas project sponsors to register their respective investment interests and requirements, thus permitting rapid access to this information by interested potential joint-venture partners in the United States and abroad.

Currently, the Opportunity Bank contains more than 1,000 investment project profiles on a broad cross-section of potential joint-venture enterprises in more than 75 countries in the developing world. The company file contains more than 4,000 potential U.S. investors.

The OPIC Opportunity Bank is now available "on-line" through Mead Data Control's Lexis/Nexis services. Please call up "OPIC" when in the "WORLD" library of Nexis. Lexis/Nexis customer support can be reached at (800) 543-6862. For more information on these programs, contact: Overseas Private Investment Corporation, 1100 New York Avenue NW, Washington, DC 20527. Telephone (202) 336-8565 or (202) 336-8799; Fax (202) 408-9859.

Foreign-Trade Zones in the United States

As an exporter you should consider the use of foreign trade zones located in over 35 communities in the U.S. These zones are considered outside customs territory. Activities such as storage, assembly, inspection, and repacking, which might otherwise be carried on overseas, are permitted.

For export operations the zones provide accelerated export status for excise tax rebates and customs drawbacks.

Contact: Dept. of Commerce, Foreign Trade Zones, Room 3716, 14th & Constitution Avenue NW, Washington, DC 20230. Speak with John DaPonte at (202) 482-2862; Fax (202) 482-0947.

156

Matchmaker Trade Delegation Program

The Department of Commerce and the SBA cosponsor the Matchmaker Trade Delegation Program. The missions are designed to introduce new-to-export or new-to-market businesses to prospective agents and distributors overseas. Commerce plans and organizes about 10 missions a year. Each Matchmaker focuses on a specific industry or group of industries. SBA provides up to $750 of assistance to the first 10 qualified small businesses that sign up for each event. Specialists from the Department of Commerce evaluate the potential of a firm's product, find and screen potential business partners, and handle logistics. An intensive trip filled with face-to-face meetings with prospective clients and in-depth briefings on the economic and business climate of the countries visited follow this.

Contact the DOC district office nearest you, or the Export Promotion Services, Dept. of Commerce at (202) 482-0692; Fax (202) 482-0178.

CHAPTER 9

Women, Minorities, and Disadvantaged

Business Development Program

The SBA acts as a prime contractor and enters into contracts with other federal departments and agencies on behalf of minority businesses. The SBA subcontracts the work to companies in the 8(a) program. These subcontracts are generally awarded on a noncompetitve or limited-competition basis.

The businesses must be at least 51 percent owned by either an individual who is a socially or economically disadvantaged citizen of the U.S. or an economically disadvantaged Indian tribe (including Alaska native corporations or native Hawaiian organizations). The SBA district offices have minority business specialists who can help in determining whether an individual is socially or economically disadvantaged. In most cases, being a woman does not, by itself, qualify an individual as a minority.

Participation in the 8(a) program qualifies businesses for several types of assistance, including management and technical assistance and government contracting and subcontracting opportunities. Contact the nearest SBA Office and ask to speak with a minority business specialist.

Contact: Small Business Administration, 409 Third Street SW, Washington, DC 20416. Telephone (202) 205-6412 or (800) 827-5722.

159

Management and Technical Assistance Program

The SBA places grants, agreements, and contracts with individuals, firms, state and local governments, and non-profit organizations to provide management and technical assistance to eligible recipients.

SBA certified 8(a) firms (see below), socially and economically disadvantaged individuals, and/or firms located in areas of high unemployment are eligible.

Booking and accounting services, production, engineering and technical advice, feasibility studies, marketing analyses and advertising expertise, limited legal services, and specialized management training are available.

Contact the nearest SBA Office (see Appendix 3 for state-by-state listings) and ask for SBA Form 641, Request for Counseling.

Contact: Small Business Administration, 409 Third Street SW, Washington, DC 20416. Telephone (202) 205-6665 or (800) 827-5722.

Office of Minority Enterprise Development

The main objective of this office is to foster business ownership by individuals who are socially and economically disadvantaged and to promote their competitive viability. The SBA has combined its efforts with those of private industry, banks, local communities, and other government agencies to meet those goals. The following programs or services are offered:

- management and technical assistance
- Section 8(a) business development program certification
- federal procurement opportunities
- bonding
- financial assistance 8(a) loan program

For more details about the 8(a) program and your eligibility requirements, call the Small Business Answer Desk at (800) 827-5722.

Contact: Small Business Administration, 409 Third Street SW, Washington, DC 20416. Phone (202) 205-6460 or Fax (202) 205-7324.

Office of Women Business Ownership

The Office of Women Business Ownership (OWBO) is the primary advocate for the interests of women business owners and provides current and potential women business owners access to the following services and programs:

- pre-business workshops
- technical, financial, and management information
- information on selling to the federal government
- access to capital

Small Loan Program

The Women's Network for Entrepreneurial Training (WNET) matches successful entrepreneurial women (mentors) with women business owners whose companies are ready to grow (protégés). Meeting one-on-one over a period of a year, mentors guide protégés through the process of achieving success in business.

Contact: Small Business Administration, 409 Third Street SW, Washington, DC 20416. Telephone (202) 205-6673.

Short-Term Lending and Bonding Assistance

The Minority Business Resource Center of the Department of Transportation operates two programs for minority, women-owned, and disadvantaged business enterprises:

- The Short-Term Lending Program, which provides you with short-term working capital at prime interest rates for transportation-related projects.

- The Bonding Assistance Program, which enables you to obtain bids, payment, and performance bonds for transportation-related projects.

For a minimal fee, these programs will also assist you in the loan packaging.

Contact: Office of Small and Disadvantaged Business Utilization (OSDBU), Department of Transportation, Minority Business Resource Center, 400 7th Street SW, Room 9414, Washington, DC 20590. Telephone (202) 366-1930; Fax (202) 366-7538.

Information Networks

The Minority Business Development Agency of the Department of Commerce has established a nationwide Business Information Network. It collects and disseminates information that is of special importance to the successful establishment and operation of minority business.

The Network is comprised of 100 Minority Business Development Centers throughout the country, and the MBDA Information Clearinghouse Center.

The Centers are linked together through a telecommunications network and use remote terminals to access automated business information systems.

Information Clearinghouse

Services available from the clearinghouse are:

- referral to sources of management and technical assistance for minority entrepreneurs.

- identification of minority vendors for government agency procurement opportunities.

- statistics and reports on agency performance.

- information about the agency and other federal support of minority assistance programs.

- referral to and use of information resources at the Clearinghouse Reference Room.

Business Development Centers

Resources available to you through the Business Development Centers are:

- The Minority Vendor PROFILE System, which is a computerized inventory of non-retail minority firms used for matching companies with opportunities.

- The X/Market database containing information on approximately 500,000 U.S. establishments in more than 950 industries, used in making decisions concerning marketing, sales, and research.

- Dun and Bradstreet Information Systems, which provides detailed financial profiles and computations useful in evaluating the performance of companies.

- DMS/ONLINE Information Systems which contains information on U.S. government prime contract awards and plans for defense and aerospace programs and for identifying direct subcontracting opportunities for minority businesses.

- The TECTRA database that identifies new technologies being used in the public sector that are thus available for commercialization.

- The Donnelly X/Census Plus database that identifies desired characteristics of a given marketing location, and can also be searched to identify a location that meets these characteristics.

- The Federal Procurement Data System reports on various aspects of federal procurement activities showing historical data on what the U.S. Government buys, and is used by many firms to develop marketing strategies.

- The F. W. Dodge Construction Information subscription service that provides information to minority businesspersons on both private and public sector construction opportunities, including post-construction services such as maintenance and landscaping.

More than 100 Minority Business Development Centers, located in areas across the country with the largest minority populations, are funded to provide management, marketing, and technical assistance to increase business opportunities for minority entrepreneurs in the United States and foreign markets.

Each center can assist existing firms as well as minority individuals interested in starting a business, and minimize their business failures.

The centers provide vital accounting, administration, business planning, construction, and marketing information. The sources of the information are major U.S. corporations, trade associations, export management companies, and federal, state and local government agencies.

They also identify minority-owned firms for contract and sub-contract opportunities with federal, state and local government agencies and the private sector. Some of the services include:

- financial statement compilation

- cost accounting
- budgeting; tax planning
- loan proposals
- cash forecasting
- office management
- forms design
- management development
- job evaluation
- performance reviews
- feasibility studies
- long-range planning
- pre-merger analysis
- operation analysis
- construction bonding and estimating
- bid preparation
- pricing policies
- advertising
- promotion
- consumer surveys
- merchandising

Businesses should contact their nearest MBDA regional office. To find it, look in the telephone book or contact Minority Business Development Agency, Department of Commerce, 14th & Constitution Avenue NW, Washington DC 20230. Telephone (202) 482-5061; Fax (202) 501-4698. Web site: www.doc. gov/resources/MBDA_info.html

Energy-Related Opportunities for Minorities

The Minority Energy Information Clearinghouse is a centralized repository and dissemination point for energy-related research data and information about energy programs and the economic impact of those programs on minorities, minority businesses, and minority educational institutions. Information is provided about the Department of Energy (DOE) and the Office of Minority Economic Impact Programs.

The clearinghouse maintains a database and provides searches and specialized information that is available through linkages with other databases of other federal agencies.

Services available from the clearinghouse are:

- referrals to sources of management and an array of technical assistance to minority business enterprises and minority educational institutions and to sources for procurement and research opportunities

- identification of minority vendors for government procurement opportunities

- statistics and performance reports on the department's activities with minority educational institutions and minority business enterprises

- information about DOE and other federal agencies' support of minority assistance programs

- identification of the research in progress in the department

- information on the impact of energy policies and programs on minorities

- regional information on socioeconomic and demographic data on minorities and their energy use patterns, and

- referrals to sources which assist in energy development programs for minority communities

The clearinghouse has a menu-driven, 24-hour bulletin board you can access from your computer. It contains numerous programs that impact minorities. The bulletin board is menu driven. It is available to you 24 hours a day. Call (800) 543-2325. The computer number is (202) 586-1561. For assistance call (202) 586-6537.

Contact: Economic Impact and Diversity Office, Department of Energy, 1000 Independence Avenue SW, Room 5B-110, Washington, DC 20585. Telephone (202) 586-7377; Fax (202) 586-3075.

Business Loans and Grants for Indians and Native Alaskans

The Bureau of Indian Affairs will provide grants, direct loans and guaranteed loans for business, agriculture, industry and housing for Indians, Alaska natives, and Indian organizations.

Any purpose that will promote economic development on or near a federal Indian reservation will be considered. Approximately $45,000,000 is available for loan guarantees. Some recent projects were construction of a Dairy Queen, a cabinet factory, and a fish processing plant.

In addition, seed money in the form of grants up to $100,000 to individuals or $250,000 to tribes is available for profit-oriented business enterprises. One recent grant was for $340,000 to purchase a pizza parlor. The business is flourishing and they have expanded into a second restaurant without government assistance.

Contact: Trust and Economic Development, Bureau of Indian Affairs, Department of the Interior, 1849 C Street NW, Room 4600, Washington, DC 20240. Telephone (202) 208-5324; Fax (202)208-3664. Web site: www.info.er.usgs.gov/doi/bureau-indian-affairs.html

Grants for Energy Usage Research

Money is available for research by minorities of energy usage such as: studies of the percentage of disposable income spent by minorities on energy compared to national averages, establishing consumption and usage patterns, and assessing potential policies and programs to be implemented by legislative and regulatory agencies.

Small and disadvantaged businesses in energy-related fields are encouraged to apply.

Contact: Department of Energy, Forrestal Building Room 5B-110, Washington, DC 20585. Telephone (202) 586-7377; Fax (202) 586-3075.

Department of Agriculture

You should contact the Department of Agriculture for information about procurement procedures. You should request information on who does the buying, the types of items bought for the various programs, and where the buying is done. Also request a directory of purchasing offices and their locations.

You may obtain a copy from the Department of Agriculture's Office of Small and Disadvantaged Business Utilization (OSDBU). Information about contracting and subcontracting opportunities is also provided.

Contact: OSDBU, Department of Agriculture, 14th & Independence Avenue SW, Room 1323-S, Washington, DC 20250. Telephone (202) 720-7117; Fax (202) 720-3001.

Department of Commerce

The OSDBU provides individual and group marketing assistance for small businesses and publishes a forecast of Commerce contracting opportunities for the current year and a complete list of previous year contracts. Requisitions are screened for possible small business set-asides and the 8(a) program prior to publication in the Commerce Business Daily (CBD).

Each year the office sets goals for contracting and subcontracting awards to small, minority, 8(a) and women-owned businesses. They also review all prime contracts for subcontracting opportunities for these firms. For Commerce, the OSDBU administers Small Business Innovation Research and R&D Goaling programs and maintains a computer listing of small concerns wishing to do business with Commerce, the U.S. Government, and prime contractors.

Contact: OSDBU, Department of Commerce, Room H6411, 14th & Constitution Avenue NW, Washington, DC 20230. Telephone (202) 482-1472; Fax (202) 482-0501.

Department of Defense

The OSDBU office is the starting point for small businesses, small disadvantaged businesses, labor surplus, and women-owned business firms desiring to do business with the DOD.

A series of publications are available to lead a business to the right contacts with the large DOD procurement system. The key publications available include Selling to the Military, Department of Defense Small Business Specialists, and Small Business Subcontracting Directory.

Contact: OSDBU, Dept. of Defense, Rm. 2A340, The Pentagon, Washington, DC 20301-3061. Telephone (703) 614-1151.

Department of Education

Contact the OSDBU for procurement information.

Request information on who does the buying, the types of items bought for the various programs, and where the buying is done. Also request a directory of purchasing offices and their locations.

Contact: OSDBU, Department of Education, Room 6000, 555 New Jersey Avenue NW, Washington, DC 20202. Telephone (202) 708-9820; Fax (202) 401-6477.

Department of Energy

The OSDBU office is the advocate and point of contact for small, disadvantaged (including 8a certified) firms, labor surplus areas, and women-owned businesses.

The office counsels such firms on how to do business with the department. They also provide the names of small/disadvantaged business specialists located in the procurement offices throughout the country who can supply more specific requirement information. Preference programs are explained and potential vendors are referred to appropriate program offices.

Contact: OSDBU, Department of Energy, 58110, 1000 Independence Avenue SW, Washington, DC 20585. Telephone (202) 586-7377.

Department of Health and Human Services

The OSDBU office develops and implements appropriate outreach programs aimed at heightening the awareness of the small business community to the contracting opportunities available within the department.

Outreach efforts include activities such as sponsoring small business fairs and procurement conferences as well as participating in group seminars, conventions, and other forums that promote the utilization of small or disadvantaged businesses as contractors.

The OSDBU provides counseling and advice to inquiring small businesses regarding their possible eligibility for special consideration under preferential procurement programs for the department employees.

Contact: OSDBU, Department of Health and Human Services, Room 513-D HHH, 200 Independence Avenue SW, Washington, DC 20201. Telephone (202) 690-7300.

Department of Housing and Urban Development (HUD)

The OSDBU office helps small, minority, and women-owned businesses understand HUD's operations and directs offerers to appropriate sources of information. OSDBU works with program offices throughout the department to develop goals for Procurement Opportunity Programs (POPs), Minority Business Enterprises (MBEs), and to encourage implementation of subcontracting plans for small and disadvantaged businesses.

It provides advice to contracting officers in complying with small and disadvantaged business utilization plans. The office participates in government/industry conferences to assist small and disadvantaged businesses and is available to give direct advice as it is needed.

In addition, the office sponsors seminars and presentations at appropriate wade shows, conferences, and policy sessions.

OSDBU develops the Department's annual Minority Business Development Plan to encourage greater participation by minority business enterprises in all HUD programs.

Contact: OSDBU, Department of Housing and Urban Development, Room 10226, 451 Seventh Street SW, Washington, DC 20410. Telephone (202) 708-1428.

Department of Justice

The OSDBU office develops and implements appropriate outreach programs aimed at heightening the awareness of the small business community to the contracting opportunities available within the department.

Outreach efforts include activities such as sponsoring small business fairs and procurement conferences as well as participating in trade group seminars, conventions, and other forums that promote the utilization of small businesses as contractors.

The OSDBU also provides counseling and advice to inquiring small businesses regarding their possible eligibility for special consideration under preferential purchasing programs which the department employs.

Contact: OSDBU, Department of Justice, 10th Street and Pennsylvania Avenue NW, Washington, DC 20530. Telephone (202) 616-0521.

Department of Labor

The Department of Labor places a fair proportion of its private sector purchases and contracts for supplies, research and development, and services (including contracts for maintenance, repairs, and construction) with small business and small disadvantaged business concerns.

The OSDBU office promotes opportunities for small or disadvantaged business concerns in acquisition programs, disseminates data about those laws administered by the department which affect contractor and subcontractor operations, and provides assistance to small and disadvantaged business concerns either directly or through coordinated interdepartmental activities.

The procurement procedures of the department are explained in a publication titled What the U.S. Department of Labor Buys. This publication contains information on who does the buying, the types of items bought for the various programs, and where the buying is done. Included is a directory of purchasing offices and their locations.

Contact: OSDBU, Department of Labor, Room N5402, 200 Constitution Avenue NW, Washington, DC 20210. Telephone (202) 219-9148.

Department of the Interior

The OSDBU office is the central point of contact for small businesses, small disadvantaged businesses, labor surplus, and woman-owned business firms desiring to do business with the department. The office is prepared to discuss the various preference programs and can assist firms in contacting appropriate department offices.

Contact: OSDBU, Department of the Interior, 1849 C Street NW, Room 2727, Washington, DC 20240. Telephone (202) 208-3493.

NASA

The OSDBU office (Code K) is responsible for the development and management of NASA programs to assist small businesses, as well as firms that are owned and controlled by socially- and economically disadvantaged individuals.

The office functionally oversees and directs the activities of corresponding offices at each installation.

The primary objective of the program is to increase the participation of small and disadvantaged businesses in NASA procurement.

The office offers individual counseling sessions to business people seeking advice on how to best pursue contracting opportunities with NASA.

Specific guidance is provided regarding procedures for getting on the bidders' mailing lists, current and planned procurement opportunities, arrangements for meetings with technical requirements personnel, and various assistance or preference programs that might be available.

Contact: OSDBU, National Aeronautics and Space Administration, Code K, Washington, DC 20546. Telephone (202) 358-2088; Fax (202) 358-3261.

Department of Transportation

The OSDBU office provides assistance, referrals, and business opportunity information resulting from the department's federally assisted projects to minority and women business enterprises through its nationwide Program Management Center Project, Hispanic Business Enterprise Project, and National Information Clearinghouse.

It provides assistance in obtaining short-term capital and bonding for minority and women business enterprises.

The MBRC contracts annually with a number of organizations to assist minority and women business enterprises in obtaining contracts from federally assisted projects.

Contact: OSDBU, Department of Transportation, Room 9414, 400 7th Street SW, Washington, DC 20590. Telephone (202) 366-1930; Fax (202) 366-7538.

Department of State

The mission of the Department of State, Office of Small and Disadvantaged Business Utilization (OSDBU) is to ensure that a fair share of the department's acquisitions are placed with small, disadvantaged, and small, women-owned firms. The OSDBU develops policies and implements actions that will enhance procurement opportunities for small, disadvantaged, and woman-owned businesses at the State Department., in accordance with public law.

The OSDBU serves as advocate, counselor, trainer, and provider of liaison services to the small business community. These services are delivered in part through participation in outreach activities including conferences sponsored by Congress, trade associations, and other federal agencies, and through one-on-one counseling as well as group training seminars. You may access office publications and other information about the program the following Web site: www.statebuy.inter.net/home.htm

Contact: OSDBU, U.S. Dept. of State, SA-6, Rm. 633, Washington, D.C. 20522-0602. Telephone (703) 875-6824; Fax (703) 875-6825.

Department of the Treasury

The OSDBU office is a central point of contact for small business, small disadvantaged business, and women-owned business firms desiring to do business with the Treasury.

OSDBU is prepared to discuss the various procurement programs and can assist firms in contacting appropriate treasury procurement personnel.

Contact: OSDBU, Department of the Treasury, Main Treasury Building, 15th and Pennsylvania Avenue NW, Room 6100 Annex, Washington, DC 20220. Telephone (202) 622-0530. Or, use the Small Business Interactive Fax Line at (202) 622-1133; Web site: www.ustreas.gov

---

GSA Assistance: Information/Marketing/Networking

The eleven General Services Administration Business Service Centers provide small and disadvantaged businesses with detailed information about Government contracting opportunities. They issue bidders' mailing list applications, furnish specifications and invitations for bids, maintain current displays of bidding opportunities, receive and safeguard bids and provide facilities for opening them, and furnish copies of publications designed to assist business representatives in doing business with the government. Copies of bid abstracts, which indicate successful bidders, other bidders, and prices bid are also available.

The GSA publication, *Doing Business With the Federal Government*, explains basic procurement policies and procedures of GSA, the Department of Defense, and 16 other agencies, and contains the locations and telephone numbers of GSA Business Service Centers and 100 GSA Small Business Information Offices across the country. It is available free from a Business Service Center. Each regional center publishes a procurement directory for the area it serves.

Contact: General Services Administration, Room 6017, 18th & F Street, NW, Washington, DC 20405. Telephone (202) 501-1794.

Programs for Women

A women-owned business is defined as "a business that is at least 51 percent owned by a woman or women, who also controls and operates it." Women are not classified as minorities for federal SBA programs; however, some states do classify women as minorities and they are therefore eligible for state programs.

The SBA maintains an ongoing nationwide women business ownership program. A Women in Business Representative represents the Women's Business Ownership Program that sponsors special programs for women business owners and those interested in starting their own businesses.

The SBA has organized a series of regional conferences that focus on such topics as business expansion, while local training programs cover general business topics of specialized areas such as home-based businesses, franchising or selling to the federal government.

The SBA has nine initiatives to help increase business ownership opportunities for women:

- improve access to credit for women-owned businesses

- fully implement the "$50,000 or less" Small Loan Program

- increase prime and subcontract awards to women-owned small businesses

- establish the Women's Network for Entrepreneurial Training (WNET) Program in 50 States

- increase representation of women on SBA's National and Regional Advisory Councils

- increase recruitment and representation of women in key management and administrative positions at SBA

- increase information about demographics, and

- support the work of the National Women's Business Council

The free publication, *A Women's Business Ownership Kit,* is available from SBA. Fact Sheet #45, Women-Owned Businesses.

The National Women's Business Council was established by the Women's Business Ownership Act of 1988, and consists of nine members, three of who are mandated by legislation and six appointed by congressional leadership. According to the act, the council reviews, reports, and recommends actions in four specific areas:

The status of women-owned businesses nationwide, including progress made and remaining barriers for assisting businesses in entering the mainstream of American economy

The roles of federal, state and local governments in assisting and promoting women-owned businesses.

Data collection procedures and the availability of data relating to women-owned businesses.

Other government initiatives which may exist relating to women-owned businesses including federal procurement

Women's Business Ownership Procurement Representatives (WOBREP)

The following federal agencies have Women-Owned Business Representatives; ask your local SBA for a local list.

Department of:

Agriculture. . . . . (202) 720-7117
Fax (202) 720-3001

Commerce. . . . . (202) 482-1472

Defense . . . . (703) 614-1151
Fax (703) 693-7014

Army. . . . . (703) 697-7753

Air Force . . . . (703) 697-4126

Navy . . . . (703) 602-2695

Defense Logistics . . . . (703) 614-1151

Education . . . . (202) 708-9820

Energy. . . . . (202) 586-7377
Fax (202) 586-5488

Health/Human Services . . . . (202) 690-7300
Fax (202) 690-8773

HUD .... (202) 708-1428
Fax (202) 708-7642
Interior .... (202) 208-3493
Justice .... (202) 616-0521
Fax (202) 616-1717
Labor.............................. (202) 219-6611
Fax (202) 219-5529
State .... (703) 875-6824
Transportation .... (202) 366-1930
Treasury............................ (202) 622-0530
Department of Veterans Affairs .... (202) 565-8124

Administrative Agencies:

Office of Personnel Management .... (202) 606-2240
Agency for International Development .... (202) 712-1500
Consumer Protection Bureau .... (202) 326-2713
Federal Maritime Commission .... (202) 523-5900
Federal Trade Commission .... (202) 326-2258
National Endowment for Humanities .... (202) 606-8494
National Science Foundation .... (703) 306-1330
Small Business Administration .... (202) 205-6665
Smithsonian Institution .... (202) 287-3331
Commodity Futures Trading Commission..... (202) 418-5170
Environmental Protection Agency .... (202) 564-4100
Federal Emergency Mgt. Agency............ (202) 646-4257
General Services Administration .... (202) 501-1021
NASA .... (202) 358-2088

National Labor Relations Board . . . . (202) 273-4040

Nuclear Regulatory Commission. . . . . (301) 415-7380

SBA Liaison Pentagon . . . . (202) 205-6459

U.S. Postal Service . . . . (202) 268-6578

CHAPTER 10

Odds and Ends

Answers to Questions on Truth In Advertising, Mail Order, Buying by Phone

The Public Reference Branch of the Federal Trade Commission answers questions concerning truthful advertising, price fixing, product warranties, truth in lending, and unfair and deceptive business acts. It offers business assistance in learning about current regulations and enforcement procedures.

Examples of common questions answered include: mail orders rules, buying by phone, FTC used car rules, getting business credit, handling customer complaints, how to advertise consumer credit, making business sense out of warranty law, and writing a care label.

Although major emphasis is placed on correcting unfair or deceptive business practices that hurt competition, businesses can also inform the commission of unfair competition from monopolistic practices including price fixing, boycotts, price discrimination, and illegal mergers and acquisitions.

Ten regional FTC offices also have been established to assist businesses and consumers.

Contact: Public Affairs, Federal Trade Commission, Room 130, 6th & Pennsylvania Avenue NW, Washington, DC 20580. Telephone (202) 326-2180 or (202) 326-2176.

Buying Surplus Goods

The Defense National Stockpile Center acquires and retains certain emergency materials in order to prevent a dependence upon foreign nations in times of national emergency. Disposals are made when materials in inventory are found to be in excess of national security needs and are usually approved by Congress.

Disposals are conducted on a nonexclusive, nondiscriminatory basis by means of sealed bids, auctions, negotiations, or other sales methods.

Every reasonable effort is made to carry out a long-term acquisition and disposal plan as formally announced. This allows industry to make developmental, research, and investment plans in anticipation of these disposals.

Contact: Defense Logistics Agency, Defense National Stockpile Center (DNSC), 8725 John J. Kingman Road, Fort Belvoir, VA 22060-6219. Telephone (703) 767-5523 or (703) 767-5525.

Buying Surplus Real Estate

The Federal Property Resource Service of the General Services Administration has the principal responsibility for surplus real property sales. It sells nearly every type of real estate found on the commercial market.

In many cases you may use a property immediately after you have been awarded the contract for purchase.

When government real property is for sale, the GSA regional office prepares a notice describing the property and how it will be sold. The notice is mailed to those who have shown an interest in buying similar property.

A computerized mailing list is maintained, and bidders' applications are available at each of GSA's Business Service Centers.

Contact: Federal Property Resources Service, General Services Administration, Office of Real Property, 1800 F Street NW, Washington, DC 20405. Telephone (800) 472-1313 or (202) 501-0204; Fax (202) 208-1722; Web site: www.gsa.gov

Commodity Futures and How They Can Be Used to Control Costs

The Communications and Education Services Office of the Commodity Futures Trading Commission offers information about commodity futures and options to assist businesses in determining their value in company purchasing and marketing strategies.

Although only a small percentage of futures trading actually leads to delivery of a commodity, futures trading can be a valuable cost control method for companies.

The commission regulates trading, offers information about futures and works with business groups on new contracts or rule changes and to help educate them about these changes.

Contact: The Communication and Education Service Office, Commodity Futures Trading Commission, 2033 K Street NW, Washington, DC 20581. Telephone (202) 418-5080 or (202) 418-5170; Fax (202) 418-5525.

Management Assistance for Rural Co-Ops

The Agricultural Cooperative Service provides research, management, and educational assistance to cooperatives to strengthen the economic position of farmers and other rural residents.

It works directly with cooperative leaders and federal and state agencies to improve organization, leadership, and operation of cooperatives and to give guidance to further development. It helps:

- farmers and other rural residents develop cooperatives to obtain supplies and services at lower costs and to get better prices for products they sell

- advises rural residents on developing existing resources through cooperative action to enhance rural living

- helps cooperatives improve services and operating efficiency

- informs members, directors, employers, and the public on how co-operatives work and benefit their members and their communities

- encourages international cooperative programs.

The agency publishes research and educational materials, and issues *Farmer Cooperatives*, a monthly periodical.

Contact: Agricultural Cooperative Service, Dept. of Agriculture, Washington, DC 20250. Telephone (202) 720-8460 or (202) 720-7558.

Where you can Get Answers on Energy Conservation and Creating Renewable Energy from Wind, Sun, Crops, and Waste

The Energy Efficiency and Renewable Energy Center (EEREC) provides basic information on the full spectrum of renewable energy technologies—solar, wind, hydroelectric, photovoltaics, geothermal, and bioconversion—and on energy conservation.

For requesters who need detailed assistance on technical problems, EEREC provides referrals to other organizations or publications.

Its purpose is to aid technology transfer by responding to public inquiries on the use of renewable energy technologies and conservation techniques for residential and commercial needs.

Once your inquiry has been initiated, the response process is basically computerized. Responses consist of a form letter with applicable publications, an immediate telephone response, an occasional original draft response, or referral to other organizations.

Contact: EEREC, Department of Energy, P.O. Box 8900, Silver Spring, MD 20907. Call toll-free (800) 523-2929; in Alaska and Hawaii call (800) 233-3071 or (202) 586-9220; Fax (202) 586-9260; Web site: www.eren.doe.gov

Help with Labor Management Relations

Two programs can provide timely information and help.

The Cooperative Labor Management Program, often identified as the Quality of Work Life Program. It is a joint effort by labor and management to work together to further their mutual interests. The aim is more satisfied and involved employees and more efficient, adaptive, and productive organizations.

The program offers a wide range of information and technical assistance services including the sponsorship of conferences and symposia, the publication of reports on organizational experiences, the preparation of educational and training materials, and the conduct of research and evaluation studies.

There is particular interest in gathering and disseminating information about innovative policies and programs developed to enhance employee participation in decision-making with regard to such issues as work organization, the work environment, technological change, and plant closures.

The division works primarily with national unions, trade associations, productivity and quality of work life centers, colleges and universities, and other organizations interested in cooperative labor relations and quality of work life programs.

For more information on this, contact: Cooperative Labor-Management Program, Department of Labor, 200 Constitution Avenue NW, Room N-5416, Washington, DC 20210. Telephone (202) 693-0122.

Mediation and Conciliation

The Mediation and Conciliation Service, which promotes labor-management peace and better labor-management relations by providing mediation assistance in disputes arising between organized employees and their employers. The service has 80 field offices in cities across the United States.

Businesses will find its services helpful in preventing or minimizing work stoppages; in helping to resolve collective bargaining disputes, by creating a better degree of understanding and cooperation between management and labor, and in assisting labor and management to select impartial arbitrators to hear and decide disputes over collective bargaining agreements.

In general, assistance from the service is limited to domestic employers involved in interstate commerce and to related labor organizations. Except as a last resort, it refrains from participation in intrastate matters or in controversies pertaining to the interpretation or application of existing contracts. Services may be provided either upon notice required by law or at the request of the involved parties.

The National Labor Relations Board must recognize the labor organizations involved as legitimate representatives of employee groups. A series of films is also available. They illustrate many of today's labor-relations problems.

Contact: Federal Mediation and Conciliation Services, 2100 K Street NW, 9th Floor, Washington, DC 20427. Telephone (202) 606-8080.

Your Friend in the Environmental Protection Agency

The EPA Small Business Ombudsman has the mission of:

- providing small businesses with easier access to the agency

- helping them comply with environmental regulations; investigating and resolving small business disputes with the agency

- increasing EPA's sensitivity to small business in developing regulations

- dealing with EPA enforcement policies, inspection procedures, and fines

- understanding water-permitting regulations and requirements for handling and treating hazardous wastes

- complying with registration procedures for pesticides

- information on financing for pollution control equipment

They answer all kinds of questions you might have. For instance, do you want to import an automobile? Ask them about emissions requirements. Need some bacterial cultures for lab research? They'll send you some from their lab. Can't understand the government's EPA rules? They'll have one of their people walk you through it.

A major responsibility of the Ombudsman is to follow closely the status and development of EPA policies affecting small businesses. The Ombudsman's office can help provide the latest information on new regulations. Several EPA brochures and reports on various small business activities and environmental issues also are available to you.

Contact: EPA Small Business Ombudsman, Environmental Protection Agency, 401 M Street SW (A-149C), Washington, DC 20460. Telephone (800) 368-5888, or from within the Washington, DC, area at (202) 564-4100.

Impartial Information on Pesticides

The National Pesticide Telecommunications Network provides a variety of impartial information about pesticides to anyone in the contiguous United States, Puerto Rico, and the Virgin Islands. It provides the medical community health professional with:

- pesticide product information
- information on recognition and management of poisonings
- toxicology and symptomatic reviews

It provides you with referrals for laboratory analyses, investigations of pesticide incidents, and emergency treatment information.

You can also be provided with pesticide information including:

- product information
- protective equipment
- safety, health and environmental effects
- cleanup procedures, disposal, and regulatory laws

Contact: National Pesticides Telecommunications Network, Environmental Protection Agency, Oregon State University, Health Sciences Center. Telephone (800) 858-7378.

Assistance Concerning Hazardous Wastes

The Hazardous Waste/Superfund Hotline was created because the Environmental Protection Agency recognized:

- that many of the firms which must comply with regulations would have difficulty understanding the regulations and the statutory requirements

- that many of these firms, particularly the smaller ones, were not in a financial position to hire consultants to answer their compliance questions

- that interested communities, including private citizens, may have questions

The Hotline serves as a central source of technical data on The Superfund Program and The Hazardous Waste Management Program.

The Hotline responds to approximately 20,000 calls per month on regulations and program activities. In addition, the Hotline telephone service accepts requests for related publications. When additional information is required, the Hotline refers callers to appropriate contacts at EPA Headquarters, EPA Regional offices, and other federal and state agencies. The Hotline telephone staff has ten information specialists with background in geology, chemistry, chemical and environmental engineering, hydro-geology, biology, and environmental science.

Contact: Hazardous Wastes/Superfund Hotline, Environmental Protection Agency, 401 M Street SW, Mail Code 05-305, Washington, DC 20460. Telephone (800) 424-9346 or in Washington, DC, (202) 554-1404.

Crime Insurance for Small Businesses

The Federal Crime Insurance Program makes crime insurance available in states where research has determined that this insurance is not fully available to you at affordable rates.

This federally subsidized program was created to make crime insurance more readily available in areas where people have been unable to buy or renew crime insurance protection from the private insurance market. Policies normally will not be canceled or non-renewed because the policyholder has reported losses.

Coverage for business is available in increments of $1,000 up to a maximum of $15,000 with your choice of the following policy coverages:

Option l: Burglary only, including safe burglary, and resulting damage

Option 2: Robbery only, inside and away from the premises, and resulting damage

Option 3: A combination of burglary and robbery in uniform and varying amounts

Contact: Federal Crime Insurance Program, Federal Insurance Administration, Federal Emergency Management Agency, 500 C Street SW, Washington, DC 20472. Telephone (800) 638-8780; within Washington, DC or Maryland (202) 646-3422.

Computer Software You Can Have

The Computer Software and Management Information Center (COSMIC) makes available to business and industry over 1,200 computer programs, inventions, discoveries, innovations, and other results of NASA project involvement, including structural analysis, thermal engineering, computer graphics, image processing, controls and robotics, artificial intelligence, and expert systems. Source code is supplied for each program along with detailed user documentation.

Contact: Commercial Development and Technology, Transfer Division, Office of Advanced Concepts and Technology (Code CU), NASA Headquarters, Washington, DC 20546. Telephone (202) 358-2320.

Audio Visual Programs Available to You

The National Audiovisual Center is the central distribution source of audiovisual programs produced by the U.S. Government.

Companies interested in using video material for training will find it useful to obtain copies of the center's descriptive catalogs and brochures.

Some of the audiovisuals available cover: alcohol and drug abuse, business/government management, consumer education, dentistry, environment/energy conservation, flight/meteorology, foreign language instruction, history, industrial safety, library/information science, medicine, nursing, science, social issues, special education, and vocational education.

Contact: Public Programs Division Education Branch, National Archives and Records Administration, 700 Pennsylvania Ave. NW Washington, DC 20408. Telephone (202) 501-5210.

Help for Businesses in Protecting Pension Plans

The Communications and Public Affairs Department of the Pension Benefit Guaranty Corporation (PBGC) will explain to you how the PBGC protects the retirement incomes of more than 38,000,000 American workers participating in more than 112,000 covered private-sector benefit pension plans.

The Corporation has assumed liability for payment of guaranteed vested pension benefits to more than 193,000 participants in approximately 1,400 plans that have terminated and are or will be trusted by the PBGC, and is currently paying monthly retirement benefits to more than 184,000 retirees. Law sets the amount of the monthly benefit that the PBGC guarantees.

The PBGC administers two pension programs—the single-employer program and the multi-employer program.

The single-employer program covers approximately 30,000,000 participants in about 110,000 single-employer pension plans.

When a single-employer plan insured by the PBGC terminates without sufficient funds to pay PBGC-guaranteed benefits, the PBGC makes up the difference, thus ensuring that all qualified participants and beneficiaries receive their guaranteed pensions.

The PBGC also assumes trusteeship of the plan and manages its assets, maintains the plan's records, and administers guaranteed benefits. The multi-employer program protects about 8,000,000 participants in more than 2,000 plans.'

Multi-employer pension plans are maintained under collective bargaining agreements and cover employees of two or more unrelated employers.

If PBGC-covered multi-employer plans become insolvent, they receive financial assistance from the PBGC to enable them to pay guaranteed benefits.

Contact: Communications and Public Affairs Department, Pension Benefit Guaranty Corporation, 1200 K Street NW, Washington, DC 20005-4026. Telephone (202) 326-4000.

How You Can Request Securities and Exchange Commission Information

The Reference Assistance Program makes available Securities and Exchange Commission information collected when exercising its mandate concerning the protection of investors and the maintenance of fair and orderly securities markets. The commission carries out its mandate under five principal laws. Under these Acts and the rules under them, publicly held corporations, broker-dealers in securities, investment companies and investment advisors must file information with the commission. Filings are designed to ensure that all material information is available to the investing public in a timely fashion.

To ensure easy public access, the commission maintains public reference rooms in New York, Chicago, and in the headquarters office in Washington. During normal business hours, you may review and photocopy all public filings.

In addition, you may order a copy by writing to the commission or telephoning the commission's contract copying service. The commission will, upon your written request, send you copies of any public documents or information. You must submit a written request stating the documents or information needed.

Further information should be obtained before writing and stating your willingness to pay the photocopying and shipping charges. Each request will take approximately two to three weeks for delivery.

For quicker service or in-depth research, the SEC advises you to employ one of the private firms that provide SEC research services. A roster of these firms and additional information is available upon your request.

Contact: Filings and Information Services, Securities and Exchange Commission, Public Reference Branch, Stop 0-18, 450 8th Street NW, Washington, DC 20549. Telephone (202) 942-8938.

When Someone Complains about Your Business

The Office of Consumer Affairs provides assistance to you to help you improve your customer relations. This office makes available to you six consumer affairs guides for your business:

- *Consumer Source Handbook*
- *Advertising, Packaging, and Labeling*
- *Managing Consumer Complaints*
- *Product Warranties and Services*
- *Credit and Financial Issues*
- *Consumer Product Safety*

They also present workshops based on these guides and have prepared manuals for use by the workshop coordinators and consumer protection agencies. Other publications useful to businesses are *Consumer Services Directory* and *Guide to Complaint Handling*.

If you want more information, write or call: Consumer Protection Bureau, Federal Trade Commission, 6th & Pennsylvania Ave. NW, Washington, DC 20580. Telephone (202) 326-3268.

How You Can Get Help on Safety without Getting into Trouble

You can receive a free confidential consultation to help recognize and correct safety and health hazards in your workplace.

A well-trained professional staff delivers the service. Most consultations take place on-site, though limited services away from the worksite are available. Primarily targeted for smaller businesses, this confidential safety and health consultation program is completely separate from the OSHA inspection effort. In addition, no citations are issued or penalties imposed.

A consultant will study an entire plant or specific designated operations and discuss the applicable OSHA standards. A consultant may also point out other safety or health risks which might not be cited under OSHA standards, but which nevertheless may pose safety or health risks. He or she may suggest other measures such as self-inspection and safety and health training to prevent future hazardous situations.

A comprehensive consultation also includes:

- appraisal of all mechanical and environmental hazards and physical work practices

- appraisal of the present job safety and health program or establishment of one

- training and assistance with implementing recommendations

Contact: OSHA Consultation Program, Occupational Safety and Health Administration, Department of Labor, Room N-3700, 200 Constitution Avenue NW, Washington, DC 20210. Telephone (202) 693-2110.

Small Business Development Centers

Alabama

University of Alabama at Birmingham . . . . . (205) 934-6760
Medical Towers Building
1717 11th Avenue South, Suite 419
Birmingham, AL 35294

Alaska

University of Alaska at Anchorage . . . . (907) 274-7232
612 W. Willoughby Ave., Suite A
Juneau, AK 99801

Arizona

Arizona SBDC Network . . . . (602) 731-8720
2411 West 14th Street, Room 132
Tempe, AZ 85281

Arkansas

University of Arkansas at Little Rock . . . . . . (501) 324-9043
Little Rock Technology Center Building
100 South Main Street, Suite 401
Little Rock, AR 72201

California

California Trade and Commerce Agency . . . . (916) 563-3210
1410 Ethan Way
Marysville, CA 95825

Colorado
Office of Business Development . . . . (970) 241-7009
Colorado Small Business Development Center
1000 Rim Drive
Durango, CO 81301

Connecticut
University of Connecticut . . . . (860) 486-4135
School of Business Administration
2 Bourn Place, U-94
Storrs, CT 06269-5094

Delaware
University of Delaware . . . . (302) 831-1555
102 MBNA America Hall   (800) 222-2279
Newark, DE 19716

District of Columbia
Howard University . . . . (202) 806-1550
Metropolitan Washington SBDC
2600 Sixth Street, NW, Room 128
Washington, D.C. 20059

Florida
University of West Florida . . . . (850) 595-5480
19 West Garden Street
Pensacola, FL 32501

Georgia
University of Georgia . . . . (706) 542-7436
Chicopee Complex, 1180 E. Broad Street
Athens, GA 30602-5412

Hawaii
Hilo (University of Hawaii at Hilo) . . . . . . (808) 933-3515
200 West Kawili Street
Hilo, HI 96720-4091

Idaho

Boise State University . . . . (208) 385-1640
College of Business, 1910 University Drive   (800) 225-3815
Boise, ID 83725

Illinois

Dept. of Commerce & Community Affairs . . (217) 524-5856
620 East Adams Street, 5th Floor
Springfield, IL 62701

Indiana

Indiana Regional SBDC . . . . (317) 261-3030
342 North Senate Ave.
Indianapolis, IN 46201

Iowa

Iowa State University . . . . (515) 292-6351
College of Business Administration   (800) 373-7232
137 Lynn Avenue
Ames IA 50014-7126

Kansas

Pittsburgh State University . . . . (316) 235-4920
1501 South Joplin
Pittsburgh, KS 66762

Kentucky

University of Kentucky . . . . (606) 257-7668
Center for Business Development
225 Business and Economics Building
Lexington, KY 40506-0034

Louisiana

University of Southwestern Louisiana . . . . . (318) 262-5344
104 University Circle
Lafayette, LA 70504

Maine
University of Southern Maine . . . . (207) 780-4420
15 Surrenden Street   (207) 780-4949
Portland, ME 04101

Maryland
Small Business Development Center . . . . . . (301) 403-8300
7100 Baltimore Ave., Suite 401
College Park, MD 30740

Massachusetts
University of Massachusetts . . . . (413) 545-6301
Room 205, School of Management
Amherst, MA 01003-4935

Michigan
Wayne State University . . . . (313) 964-1798
2727 Second Avenue
Detroit, MI 48201

Minnesota
Department of Trade and . . . . (612) 297-5770
Economic Development
500 Metro Square, 121 Seventh Place East
St. Paul, MN 55101-2146

Mississippi
University of Mississippi . . . . (601) 232-5001
Old Chemistry Building, Suite 216
University, MS 38677

Missouri
University of Missouri . . . . (573) 882-0344
1205 University Ave.
Columbia, MO 65211

Montana
Montana Department of Commerce . . . . . . (406) 444-4780
1424 Ninth Avenue
Helena, MT 59620

Nebraska
University of Nebraska at Omaha . . . . (402) 554-2521
College of Business Administration Building
60th & Dodge Streets, Room 407
Omaha, NE 68182

Nevada
University of Nevada at Reno . . . . (702) 784-1717
College of Business Administration, Room 411
Reno, NV 89557-0100

New Hampshire
University of New Hampshire . . . . (603) 862-2200
108 McConnell Hall
Durham, NH 03824

New Jersey
Rutgers University . . . . (973) 353-1927
Graduate School of Management
49 Bleeker Street
Newark, NJ 07102

New Mexico
University of New Mexico . . . . (505) 925-8500
280 La Entrada
Los Lunas, NM 87031

New York
State University of New York (SUNY) . . . . (518) 4453-9567
1 Pinnacle Place   (800) 732-SBDC
Albany, NY 12203

North Carolina
University of North Carolina . . . . (919) 715-7272
333 Fayetteville Street, Suite 1150   (800) 258-0862
Raleigh, NC 27601

North Dakota
University of North Dakota   . . . . (701) 772-8502
202 North 3rd Street   (800) 445-7232
Grand Forks, ND 58203

Ohio
Ohio Department of Development   . . . . . . (614) 225-6910
37 North High Street, P.O. Box 1001
Columbus, OH 43215

Oklahoma
Southeastern State University . . . . (405) 924-0277
517 University   (800) 522-6154
Durant, OK 74701

Oregon
Lane Community College   . . . . (541) 726-2250
44 W. Broadway, Suite 501
Eugene, OR 97401

Pennsylvania
University of Pennsylvania   . . . . (215) 898-1219
The Wharton School, 423 Vance Hall
3733 Spruce Street
Philadelphia, PA 19104-6374

Puerto Rico
University of Puerto Rico at Mayaguez   . . . . (809) 834-3590
Building B, Second Floor, Box 5253-College Station
Mayaguez, PR 00681

Rhode Island

Bryant College SBDC . . . . (401) 232-6111
1150 Douglas Pike
Smithfield, RI 02917-1284

South Carolina

University of South Carolina . . . . (803) 777-5118
College of Business Administration
1710 College Street
Columbia, SC 29208

South Dakota

University of South Dakota . . . . (605) 677-5498
School of Business, Patterson Hall 115
414 East Clarke Street
Vermillion, SD 57069

Tennessee

University of Tennessee . . . . (901) 678-2500
South Campus (Get Well Road) Building #1
Memphis, TN 38152

Texas

Dallas County Community College . . . . . . (214) 747-1300
2050 North Stemmons Fwy.
Dallas, TX 75215

Utah

University of Utah . . . . (801) 957-3480
1623 S. State St.
Salt Lake City, UT 84115

Vermont

Vermont Technical College . . . . (802) 728-9101
P.O. Box 422   (800) 464-SBDC
Randolf, VT 05060-0422

Virginia
George Mason University, SBDC . . . . (703) 277-7700
4031 University Ave., Suite 200
Fairfax, VA 22030

Virgin Islands
University at the Virgin Islands . . . . (809) 776-3206
8000 Nisky Center, Suite 202
Charlotte Amalie, St. Thomas, VI 00802-5804

Washington
Washington State University . . . . (509) 3358-7765
College of Business and Economics
601 W. First St.
Spokane, WA 99202

West Virginia
West Virginia Development Office . . . . (304) 558-2960
950 Kanawha Boulevard
Charleston, WV 25301

Wisconsin
University of Wisconsin . . . . (608) 263-7680
975 University Ave., Room 3260
Madison, WI 53706

Wyoming
Small Business Development Center . . . . . . (307) 234-6683
U.S. Small Business Administration
111 W. Second St., Suite 502
Casper, WY 82601

Small Business Administration Field Offces

Alabama

2121 8th Avenue N, Suite 200
Birmingham, AL 35203-2398 . . . . (205) 731-1344

Alaska

222 W. 8th Avenue, Room A36
Anchorage, AK 99513-7559 . . . . (907) 271-4022

Arizona

2828 N. Central Avenue, Suite 800
Phoenix, AZ 85004-1025 . . . . (602) 640-2316

Arkansas

2120 Riverfront Drive, Suite 100
Little Rock, AR 72202 . . . . (501) 324-5871

California

2719 N. Air Fresno Drive, Suite 107
Fresno, CA 93727-1547 . . . . (209) 487-5791

330 N. Brand Blvd, Suite 1200
Glendale, CA 91203-2304 . . . . (818) 552-3210

550 West "C" Street
San Diego, CA 92101 . . . . (619) 557-7250

455 Market Street, 6th Floor
San Francisco, CA 94105-2420 . . . . (415) 744-6820

200 West Santa Ana Blvd., Suite 700
Santa Ana, CA 92701 . . . . (714) 550-7420

Colorado
721 19th Street, Room 426
Denver, CO 80202-2599 . . . . (303) 844-2607

Connecticut
Federal Bldg. 330 Main Street, 2nd Floor
Hartford, CT 06106 . . . . (203) 240-4700

District of Columbia
1110 Vermont Avenue NW, Suite 900
Washington, D.C. 20036 . . . . (202) 606-4000

Florida
100 South Biscayne Blvd.
Miami, FL 33131 . . . . (305) 536-5521

7825 Bay Meadows Way, Suite 100-B
Jacksonville, FL 32256-7504 . . . . (904) 443-1900

Georgia
233 Peachtree St. NE, Suite 1900
Atlanta, GA 30303 . . . . (404) 331-0100

Guam
400 Route 8
Mongmong, GM 96927 . . . . (671) 472-7297

Hawaii
300 Ala Moana, Room 2213
Honolulu, HI 96850-4981 . . . . (808) 541-2990

Idaho

1020 Main Street, Suite 290
Boise, ID 83702-5745 . . . . (208) 334-1696

Illinois

500 West Madison Street, Room 1250
Chicago, IL 60661-2511 . . . . (312) 353-4528

Indiana

429 North Pennsylvania Street, Suite 100
Indianapolis, IN 46204-1873 . . . . (317) 226-7272

Iowa

215 Fourth Avenue SE, Suite 200
Cedar Rapids, IA 52402-1806 . . . . (319) 362-6405

Room 749, New Federal Bldg. 210 Walnut Street
Des Moines, IA 50309 . . . . (515) 284-4422

Kansas

100 E. English Street, Suite 510
Wichita, KS 67202 . . . . (816) 374-6708

Kentucky

Room 188, Federal Bldg.
600 Martin Luther King Place
Louisville, KY 40202 . . . . (502) 582-5971

Louisiana

365 Canal Street, Suite 3100
New Orleans, LA 70130 . . . . (504) 589-6685

Maine

Room 512, Federal Bldg, 40 Western Avenue
Augusta, ME 04330 . . . . (207) 622-8378

Maryland
10 S. Howard Street, Suite 6200
Baltimore MD 21201-2565 . . . . (410) 962-4392

Massachusetts
10 Causeway Street, Room 265
Boston MA 02222-1093 . . . . (617) 565-5590

Michigan
477 Michigan Avenue, Room 515
Detroit, MI 48226 . . . . (313) 226-6075

Minnesota
100 North 6th Street, Suite 610
Minneapolis, MN 55403-1563 . . . . (612) 370-2324

Mississippi
101 West Capitol Street, Suite 400
Jackson, MS 39201 . . . . (601) 965-4378

Missouri
323 W. 8th Street, Suite 501
Kansas City, MO 64105 . . . . (816) 374-6708

815 Olive Street, Room 242
St. Louis, MO 63101 . . . . (314) 539-6600

Montana
301 S. Park Avenue, Room 334
Helena, MT 59626-0054 . . . . (406) 441-1081

Nebraska
11145 Mill Valley Road
Omaha, NE 68154 . . . . (402) 221-4691

Nevada
300 Las Vegas Blvd. South, Suite 1100
Las Vegas, NV 89101 . . . . (702) 388-6611

New Hampshire
143 N. Main Street, Room 202
Concord, NH 03301-1257 . . . . (603) 225-1400

New Jersey
Two Gateway Center
Newark, NJ 07102 . . . . (201) 645-2434

New Mexico
625 Silver Street, Room 320
Albuquerque, MN 87102 . . . . (505) 246-7909

New York
Room 1311, Federal Bldg. 111 West Huron St.
Buffalo, NY 14202 . . . . 716) 846-4301

26 Federal Plaza, Room 3100
New York, NY 10278 . . . . (212) 264-4354

401 S. Salina St.
Syracuse, NY 13202 . . . . (315) 471-9393

North Carolina
200 North College Street, Suite A2015
Charlotte, NC 28202-2137 . . . . (704) 344-6563

North Dakota
Room 219, Federal Bldg.
657 2nd Avenue NW
Fargo, ND 58108-3086 . . . . (701) 239-5131

Ohio
1111 Superior, Suite 360
Cleveland, OH 44144-2507 . . . . (216) 522-4180

2 Nationwide Plaza, Suite 1400
Columbus, OH 43215-2592 . . . . (614) 469-6860

Oklahoma
210 Park Avenue, Suite 1300
Oklahoma City, OK 73102 . . . . (405) 231-5521

Oregon
1515 S.W. Fifth Avenue, Suite 1050
Portland, OR 97201-5494 . . . . (503) 326-2682

Pennsylvania
100 Liberty Ave.
Pittsburgh, PA 15222 . . . . (412) 395-6560

Puerto Rico & Virgin Islands
252 Ponce De Leon Ave.
Hato Rey, PR 00918 . . . . (787) 766-5572

Rhode Island
380 Westminster Mall, 5th Floor
Providence, RI 02903 . . . . (401) 528-4561

South Carolina
1835 Assembly Street, Room 358
Columbia, SC 29202 . . . . (803) 765-5377

South Dakota
110 S. Phillips Avenue, Suite 200
Sioux Falls, SD 57102-1109 . . . . (605) 330-4243

St. Croix Post-of-Duty
3013 Goldenrock, Suite 165

St. Croix, VI 00820 . . . . (809) 778-5380
St. Thomas Post-of-Duty

3800 Crown Bay
St. Thomas, VI 00802 . . . . (809) 774-8530

Tennessee
50 Vantage Way, Suite 201
Nashville, TN 37228-1500 . . . .(615) 736-5881

Texas
4300 Amon Carter Blvd, Suite 114
Fort Worth, TX 76155 . . . . (817) 885-6500

10737 Gateway West, Suite 320
El Paso, TX 79935 . . . . (915) 540-5586

222 E. Van Buren Street, Room 500
Harlingen, TX 78550 . . . . (956) 427-8533

9301 SW Freeway, Suite 550
Houston, TX 77074-1591 . . . . (713) 773-6500

1205 Texas Avenue
Lubbock, TX 79401 . . . . (806) 472-7462

727 E. Durango, 5th Floor
San Antonio, TX 78206 . . . . (210) 472-5900

Utah
Room 2237, Federal Bldg.
125 S. State Street
Salt Lake City, UT 84138-1195 . . . . (801) 524-5804

Vermont
Room 205, Federal Bldg.
87 State Street
Montpelier, VT 05602 . . . .(802) 828-4422

Virginia
400 N. 8th Street, Suite 1150
Richmond, VA 23229 . . . . (804) 771-2400

Washington

1200 Sixth Avenue, Suite 1700
Seattle, WA 98101-1128 . . . . (206) 553-7310

801 W. Riverside Ave.
Spokane, WA 99201 . . . . (509) 353-2809

West Virginia

320 Pike, Suite 330
Clarksburg, WV 26301 . . . . (304) 623-5631

Wisconsin

740 Regent Street
Madison, WI 53715 . . . . (608) 264-5261

Wyoming

Room 4001, Federal Bldg. 100 E. "B" Street
Casper, WY 82602-2839 . . . . (307) 261-6500

Appendix 3

Quick Reference Guide

Executive Office of The President
Personnel Locator . . . . (202) 395-1088
Press Office . . . . (202) 456-7150
Public Comments . . . . (202) 456-1111
Visitors' Office . . . . (202) 456-2322

Department of Agriculture
Personnel Locator . . . . (202) 720-8732
Communications . . . . (202) 720-4623

Department of Commerce
Personnel Locator . . . . (202) 482-2000
Public Affairs . . . . (202) 482-4883

Department of Defense
Personnel Locator . . . . (703) 545-6700
Public Affairs . . . . (703) 697-5131

Department of Education
Personnel Locator . . . . (202) 401-2000
Public Affairs . . . . (202) 401-1576
Public Information . . . . (202) 401-2000

Department of Energy
Personnel Locator . . . . (202) 586-5000
Public Information . . . . (202) 586-5575

Department of Health And Human Services
Personnel Locator . . . . (202) 619-0257
Public Affairs . . . . (202) 690-7850

Department of Housing & Urban Development
Personnel Locator .... (202) 708-1112
Public Affairs .... (202) 708-0980

Department of Interior
Personnel Locator & Info .... (202) 208-3100
Communications .... (202) 208-6416

Department of Justice
Personnel Locator .... (202) 514-2000
Public Affairs .... (202) 514-2007

Department of Labor
Personnel Locator .... (202) 219-5000
Public Affairs .... (202) 219-7316

Department of State
Personnel Locator ....(202) 647-4000
Public Information ....(202) 647-6575

Department of Transportation
Personnel Locator ....(202) 366-4000
Public Affairs ....(202) 366-5580

Department of Treasury
Personnel Locator ....(202) 622-2111
Public Affairs ....(202) 622-2960

Department of Veterans Affairs
Personnel Locator ....(202) 273-5400
Public Affairs ....(202) 273-6000

Commission on Civil Rights
Personnel Locator ....(202) 376-8364
Public Affairs ....(202) 376-8312

Commodity Futures Trading Commission
Personnel Locator ....(202) 418-5000
Public Affairs ....(202) 418-5080

Consumer Product Safety Commission
Personnel Locator . . . . (301) 504-0990
Public Affairs . . . . (301) 504-0580

Corporation for National Service
Personnel Locator . . . . (202) 606-5000 Ext.332
Public Affairs . . . . (202) 606-5000 Ext.184
Toll-free . . . . (800) 424-8867

Environmental Protection Agency
Personnel Locator . . . . (202) 260-2090
Public Affairs . . . . (202) 260-4355

Equal Employment Opportunity Commission
Communications & Legislative Affairs . . . (202) 663-4900

Farm Credit Administration
Personnel Locator . . . . (703) 883-4135

Congressional and Public Affairs . . . . (703) 883-4056
Federal Communications Commission
Personnel Locator . . . . (202) 418-0200
Public Affairs . . . . (202) 418-0500

Federal Deposit Insurance Corporation
Personnel Locator . . . . (202) 942-3626
Press Office . . . . (202) 898-6993

Federal Emergency Management Agency
Personnel Locator . . . . (202) 646-2500
Public Affairs . . . . (202) 646-4600

Federal Labor Relations Authority
Personnel Locator . . . . (202) 482-6660
Public Info & Publications . . . . (202) 482-6560

Federal Maritime Commission
Personnel Locator . . . . (202) 523-5773
Public Affairs . . . . (202) 523-5725

Federal Mediation & Conciliation Service
Personnel Locator .... (202) 606-5460
Public Information .... (202) 606-8080

Federal Mine Safety & Health
Review Commission .... (202) 653-5663

Federal Reserve System
Personnel Locator .... (202) 452-3000
Public Affairs .... (202) 452-3204

Federal Trade Commission
Personnel Locator .... (202) 326-2000
Public Affairs .... (202) 326-2180

General Services Administration
Personnel Locator .... (202) 708-5082
Public Affairs .... (202) 501-0705

International Trade Commission
Personnel Locator .... (202) 205-2000
Public Affairs .... (202) 205-1819

Merit Systems Protection Board
Personnel Locator .... (202) 653-6772
Public Information .... (202) 653-7200

National Aeronautics & Space Administration
Personnel Locator .... (202) 358-0000
Public Affairs .... (202) 358-1898

National Archives & Records Administration
.... (202) 501-5400

National Credit Union Administration
Public Affairs .... (202) 518-6510

National Labor Relations Board
Personnel Locator .... (202) 273-1000
Information .... (202) 273-1991

National Transportation Safety Board
Public Affairs .... (202) 314-6100
Personnel Locator .... (202) 314-6000

Nuclear Regulatory Commission
Personnel Locator .... (301) 415-7000
Public Affairs .... (301) 415-8200

Occupational Safety & Health Review Commission
Personnel Locator .... (202) 606-5390
Public Affairs .... (202) 606-5398

Office of Personnel Management
Personnel Locator .... (202) 606-2424
Public Affairs .... (202) 606-1800

Peace Corps
Personnel Locator .... (202) 692-1315
Public Affairs .... (202) 692-2236

Railroad Retirement Board .... (312) 751-4915
Securities & Exchange Commission
Personnel Locator .... (202) 942-4144
Public Affairs .... (202) 942-0020

Selective Service System
Personnel Locator .... (703) 605-4000
Public Affairs .... (703) 605-4100

Small Business Administration
Personnel Locator .... (202) 205-6600
Public Information .... (202) 205-6740

Social Security Administration
Personnel Locator .... (410) 965-2982

Tennessee Valley Authority
Personnel Locator .... (423) 632-2101

U.S. Postal Service
Personnel Locator .... (202) 268-2000
Media Relations .... (202) 268-2155

Index

Index

Index

Index

Truck, 82

Trucking, 82

Trust and Economic Development, 167

Truth in lending and advertising, 181

U

U.S. Foreign Trade Highlights, 147

Unfair foreign trade practice, 154

Unfair or deceptive business, practices, 181

Urban Design, grants for, 122

Urban Rehabilitation, Office of, 122

V

Veterans, loans for, 106

Veterans Administration, 66

Video of Art of Dance, grants for, 120

Vietnam veterans, 106

Visual Artists grants for, 121

Vocational and Adult Education, Office of, 123

W

Waste products, conversion to energy, 184

Water Resources Research, grants for, 124

Weight and Measures Office, 71

Wind energy technology, 184

Women, 161, 176, 178

Women business enterprises, 159

Women's Business Ownership, 161

Women, grants for, 111

Wood products, 48

Working Capital Guarantee, Program, 104

World Traders Data Reports, 149

Writers, grants for, 121

Writers, grants for residencies for 121

X

X/Market database, 163

XIS, 139

Y

Youth Project Loan, 86

More Free Stuff!!

Take advantage of our web site at
www.pumapublishing.com
for additional free material such as:

State Financing Programs

- State and local economic development agencies are often easier to deal with than banks or the federal government. We've complied a list of each state financial programs and hyperlinks you can click on to get to your state's economic development web site.

Internet Business Resources

- Here is a compilation of resources for small business we've found useful.

Free Business Plan Software

- You'll be needing a business plan soon if you're just starting out.

  You can download an outline and financial spreadsheet of a sample plan, substitute your data, and *VIOLA!* an instant business plan. It is available in a variety of Windows/Macintosh application formats.

  Use as a stand alone or in combination with our book *The Instant Business Plan* ISBN 0-940673-42-8